July 2001

Ian,

   I hope you get to dive in
as many of these places as you
can!

      love you always

         Linda

         x

TOP DIVE SITES *of the Indian Ocean*

TOP DIVE SITES

of the

Indian Ocean

CONSULTANT   JACK JACKSON

NEW
HOLLAND

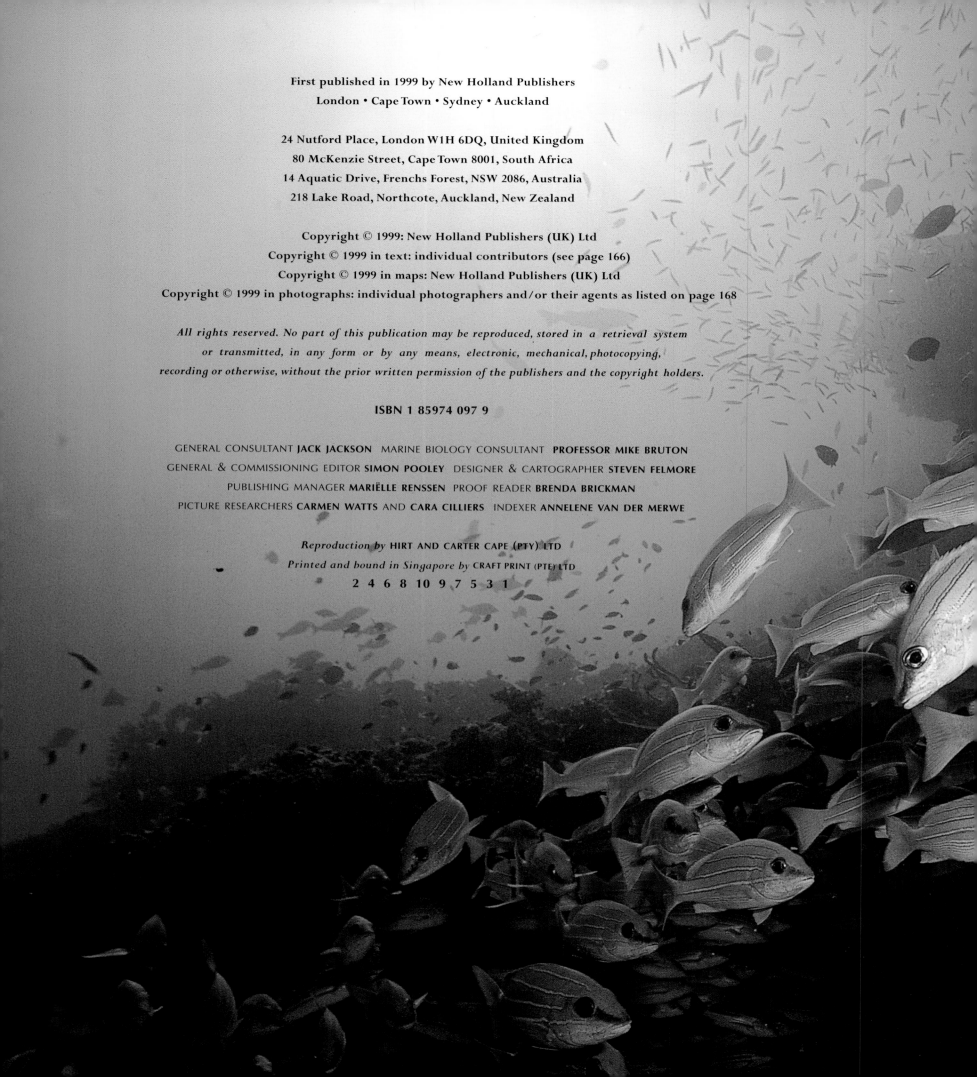

First published in 1999 by New Holland Publishers
London • Cape Town • Sydney • Auckland

24 Nutford Place, London W1H 6DQ, United Kingdom
80 McKenzie Street, Cape Town 8001, South Africa
14 Aquatic Drive, Frenchs Forest, NSW 2086, Australia
218 Lake Road, Northcote, Auckland, New Zealand

ISBN 1 85974 097 9

GENERAL CONSULTANT **JACK JACKSON** MARINE BIOLOGY CONSULTANT **PROFESSOR MIKE BRUTON**
GENERAL & COMMISSIONING EDITOR **SIMON POOLEY** DESIGNER & CARTOGRAPHER **STEVEN FELMORE**
PUBLISHING MANAGER **MARIËLLE RENSSEN** PROOF READER **BRENDA BRICKMAN**
PICTURE RESEARCHERS **CARMEN WATTS** AND **CARA CILLIERS** INDEXER **ANNELENE VAN DER MERWE**

Reproduction by HIRT AND CARTER CAPE (PTY) LTD
Printed and bound in Singapore by CRAFT PRINT (PTE) LTD
2 4 6 8 10 9 7 5 3 1

CONTENTS

30°

GULF OF AQABA

EGYPT

SAUDI ARABIA

23.5° N

RED SEA

SUDAN

60°

ARABIAN SEA

ERITREA   YEMEN

INDIA

GULF OF ADEN

CARLSBERG RIDGE

LAKSHADWEEP ARCHIPELAGO

SRI LANKA

KENYA

MALDIVES

0°

TANZANIA

Pemba Island

SEYCHELLES

MADAGASCAR PLATEAU

Chagos ARCHIPELAGO

MID-INDIAN RIDGE

COMOROS

INDIAN OCEAN

MADAGASCAR

Bazaruto Archipelago

MOZAMBIQUE   Bassas da India

23.5° S

Ponta do Ouro

Sodwana Bay

SOUTH AFRICA

Aliwal Shoal Protea Banks

INDIAN RIDGE

SOUTHEAST INDIAN RIDGE

| 0 | 500 | 1000 | 1500 | 2000 | 2500 Miles |

| 0 | 500 | 1000 | 1500 | 2000 | 2500 | 3000 | 3500 Kilometres |

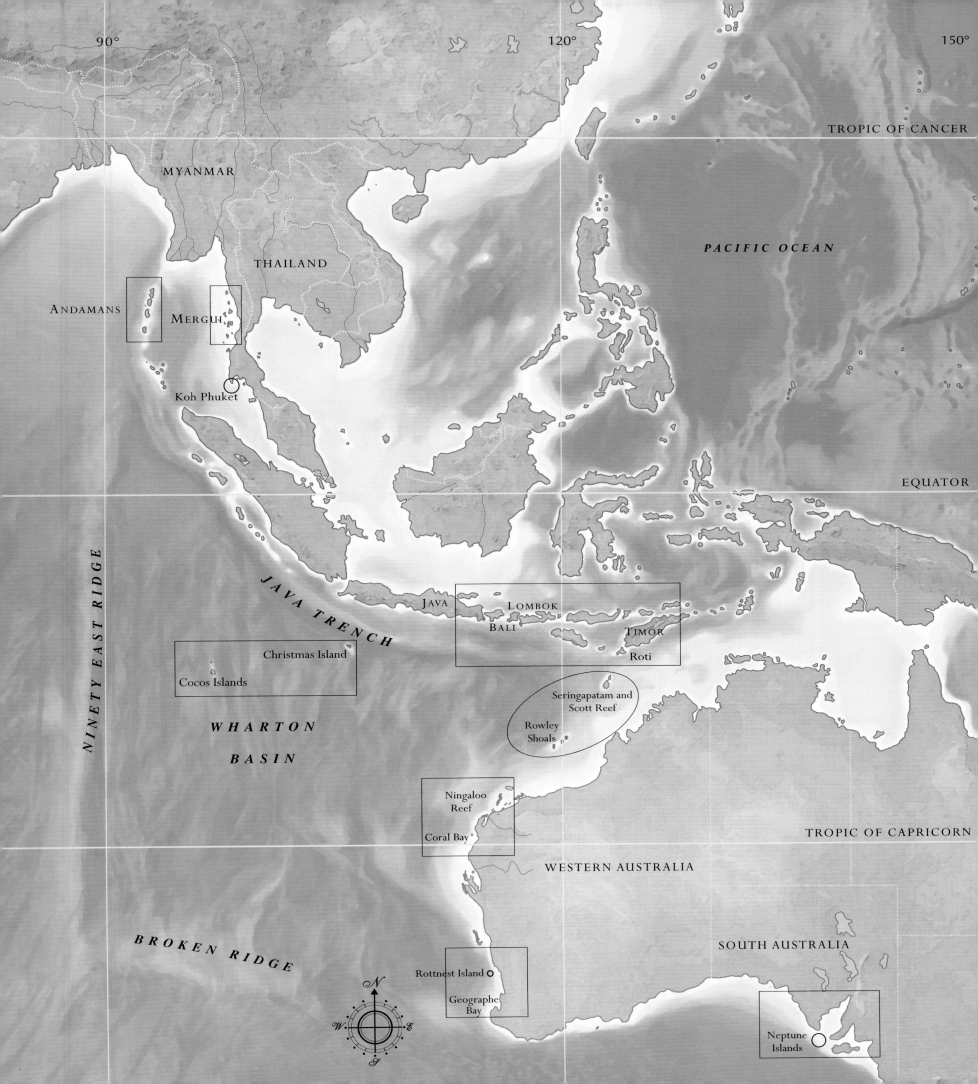

90° 120° 150°

TROPIC OF CANCER

MYANMAR

THAILAND

PACIFIC OCEAN

ANDAMANS

MERGUI

Koh Phuket

EQUATOR

NINETY EAST RIDGE

JAVA TRENCH

Java

LOMBOK

BALI

TIMOR

Roti

Christmas Island

Cocos Islands

WHARTON

BASIN

Seringapatam and
Scott Reef

Rowley
Shoals

Ningaloo
Reef

Coral Bay

TROPIC OF CAPRICORN

WESTERN AUSTRALIA

BROKEN RIDGE

SOUTH AUSTRALIA

N

Rottnest Island

Geographe
Bay

W E

S

Neptune
Islands

*T*he choice of top dive sites is always likely to stimulate a spirited argument. Most divers prefer the warm water, dramatic coral reefs, copious fish and invertebrate life, and clear visibility of tropical seas. But some prefer fast drift dives, some wreck dives, others searching for life in the shallows. In compiling this selection of top sites we have taken into account these parameters, together with the accessibility of the location (bar a couple of aspirational sites) and, where available, accompanying interesting sites on land.

Bass Strait, the Indian Ocean covers an area of 73,556,000km² (28,400,000 sq. miles).

The African, Indian and Antarctic tectonic plates converge in the Indian Ocean as the mid-oceanic ridge. Shaped like an inverted 'Y', the stem runs north and then west as the Carlsberg Ridge to join the rift system of the Red Sea. One arm extends around southern Africa to connect with the Mid-Atlantic Ridge, while the other extends south around Australia to connect with the East Pacific Rise. This underwater chain of mountains repre-

water and the outflows of rivers laden with silt create barriers between shallow water communities.

WINDS AND CURRENTS

The northern Indian Ocean is unique among oceans in that its current pattern changes twice in each year. In winter, high pressure over northern Asia from cold, falling air results in the northeast monsoon and northeast-to-southwest winds and currents. The winds blow from October until April, generating the North Equatorial Current, which carries

THE INDIAN OCEAN

The Indian Ocean is the third-largest body of water in the world after the Pacific and Atlantic Oceans; larger than the Antarctic Ocean, it covers roughly 20 per cent of the Earth's water surface. No natural boundary separates the Indian Ocean from the Atlantic, Antarctic and Pacific Oceans. The 20° meridian east of Greenwich, through Cape Agulhas at the southern end of Africa, is used to denote separation from the Atlantic Ocean to the west. The 147° meridian east of Greenwich marks the easternmost limit of its extent, where it meets the Pacific Ocean off southern Australia. The Antarctic Ocean includes all oceanic areas south of latitude 55° South.

Bordered in the west by Africa and the Arabian Peninsula, in the north by southern Asia, in the east by the Malay Peninsula, Indonesia and Australia, and in the south by the Antarctic Ocean, the Indian Ocean is extremely varied in its coastal habitat, reef development and species diversity.

Including the Gulf of Aqaba, the Red Sea, the Arabian (Persian) Gulf, the Gulf of Oman, the Arabian Sea, the Bay of Bengal, the Straits of Malacca, the Great Australian Bight and the

sents strong volcanic activity at the centre of sea floor spreading.

At the Red Sea, the northern part of Africa is actively moving apart from Arabia, and in (geological) time it will probably be wide enough to be an ocean. By contrast the Arabian Plate, one of the earth's smallest tectonic plates, is moving to the northeast and disappearing under the Asian Plate below the Zagros Mountains of Iran. Eventually, the Arabian Gulf is likely to close off completely.

Off Indonesia the Java Trench, 7450m (24,442ft) deep, is thought to mark the line of subduction where the Australian Plate goes below the Eurasian Plate. This plate movement has only been active for the last two million years and the related volcanic activity is high. The eruption of Krakatoa in 1883 was heard as far away as Australia.

In recent geological time the sea levels in the Indian Ocean have been raised or lowered for various reasons, such that many marine populations have been split up and isolated. If this isolation continued for long enough, then some of these populations are likely to have developed into separate species. Where there are remote islands, they have also created many situations for isolating shallow water organisms. Large areas of very deep

water towards the coast of Africa. From May until October, low atmospheric pressure over southwest Asia from hot, rising air results in the southwest monsoon, and southwest-to-northeast winds prevail. In the Arabian Sea, the southwest monsoon brings heavy rain to the Indian subcontinent.

In the southern hemisphere, the winds are generally milder, but summer storms near Mauritius can be severe. Trade winds drive a broad, circular system of currents (a gyre) of warm water anti-clockwise. The South Equatorial current carries water towards Africa, where the portion not connected with the monsoon wind system curls south below Madagascar and reinforces the Agulhas Current which flows south along the east coast of Africa. In winter this combined southward flowing current can reach speeds of 180km (112 miles) per day along the edge of South Africa's continental shelf. At this speed it can more than double the height of waves travelling north from

---

ABOVE (left to right) *A skunk clownfish* (Amphiprion akallopisos); *a yellow-eyed combtooth blenny* (Ecsenius melarchus); *Bullock's nudibranchs* (Chromodoris bullocki); Chromodoris magnifica *nudibranchs*.

storms in the Antarctic Ocean. The area is well known as a hazard to shipping, and divers must put up with a high-voltage experience as dive boats are launched through heavy surf.

Tropical cyclones occur during May/June and October/November in the north of the Indian Ocean and January/February in the south. When the monsoon winds change, cyclones sometimes strike the shores of the Arabian Sea and the Bay of Bengal.

In days gone by, sailing ships plying the important India and Southeast Asia trade route to return

skeleton that, fused together with others and with rubble debris, forms the reef. These corals require warm, clear water with maximum exposure to sunlight for survival so, except for where the water is unusually warm for its geographical area, true reefs grow only in tropical seas. However, the clear seas found typically in the tropics are very poor in nutrients. Most stony corals make up for this by living in symbiosis with algae and absorbing the nutrients that they excrete. In recent years, higher water temperatures related to the El Niño-Southern

Pacific covered their cold, nutrient-rich eastern coastal waters, and as a result the fish died or left the area in search of food. However, torrential rains fell on the normally arid land, the desert turned green and farmers produced record crops. This warming started around Christmas so they called the event El Niño, Spanish for 'the boy child', referring to the infant Jesus Christ.

Under normal conditions, the vast Pacific Ocean receives more solar energy than any other Ocean. This, together with the easterly trade winds, con-

with rugs, spices, silks and tea, made full use of the monsoon 'trade winds'. They made the eastward journey with the help of the winds of the Southwest Monsoon and then timed their return departure to between November and March to gain the winds and currents produced by the Northeast Monsoon. Nowadays, ships have a much easier passage through the Suez Canal.

CORAL REEFS

Today's coral reefs have developed as a result of rising sea levels after the last Ice Age. A rate of expansion of one metre (3.28ft) can take anywhere between 300 and 3000 years but natural forces such as cyclones or earthquakes can destroy these reefs in seconds. The ravages of humankind may take a little longer but the result is just the same.

Coral reefs are mainly constructed by stony corals; individual coral animals secrete a limestone

ABOVE (left to right) *A tiger grouper* (Epinephelus posteli) *resting on a bed of hard corals; a loggerhead turtle* (Caretta caretta); *a* Chromodon's burrei *sea slug; pink anemonefish* (Amphiprion perideraion).

Oscillation phenomenon have caused stress to many anemones, clams and fast-growing stony corals and they have responded by expelling their symbiotic algae. The result is bleaching. If the water temperatures do not return to normal fairly quickly then these animals will die.

EL NIÑO AND LA NIÑA

Once thought to only affect a narrow strip of water off Peru, it is now recognized that the effects on the world's weather related to El Niño and its counterpart, La Niña, extend throughout the Pacific Rim to eastern and southern Africa.

Normally accompanied by a change in atmospheric circulation called the Southern Oscillation, the El Niño-Southern Oscillation (ENSO) phenomenon is one of the main sources of changes in the world's weather and climate. In 1997/98 the sea-surface temperatures in most tropical seas were particularly high; divers noticed large-scale coral bleaching and the sharks migrated to deeper, colder water. Nearly every region on Earth felt El Niño's effect in some way.

In the late 19th century, Peruvian fishermen noticed that every three to seven years, a layer of warm, nutrient-depleted water from the west

tributes to the ENSO process. These trade winds push water towards the western Pacific such that the sea level in the Philippines is normally some 60cm (23in) higher than that on the southern coast of Panama. The westward-flowing water thus remains near to the surface and heats up. This causes the western Pacific to have the warmest sea-surface temperatures on earth, usually above 28°C (82°F). The warm surface water pushes down the thermocline, causing the air pressure to drop so that moist air rises. As a result, frequent thunderstorms and some of the world's heaviest rainfall occur in Northern Australia, Papua New Guinea and Indonesia. In the eastern Pacific, the water is cold and the air pressure is high. The trade winds, blowing from east to west, push sun-warmed surface waters westward and expose cold water to the surface in the east.

When an El Niño occurs, sea-surface temperatures in the southeastern tropical Pacific are unusually high. The easterly trade winds in the central and western Pacific collapse or even reverse and the warm waters of the western Pacific flow back eastward. As a result, sea-surface temperatures increase significantly off the western coast of South America.

As this happens, the wet weather conditions normally present in the western Pacific move to the east, and the arid conditions common to the eastern Pacific appear in the west. This brings heavy rains to South America, droughts and bush fires in Australia and droughts in southeastern Asia, India, and southern Africa, a factor that exacerbated the spate of forest fires and smoke haze over Indonesia and Malaysia in 1998.

El Niño is often called 'a warm event'. When the opposite occurs – unusually cold ocean temperatures in the eastern Equatorial Pacific – it is called a 'cold event', referred to as La Niña, meaning 'The Little Girl'. The impacts on global climate are the opposite to those of El Niño.

WESTERN INDIAN OCEAN

South Africa's southern coastline has waters as cold and rough as those around northern Europe, but further up the east coast are the world's most southerly coral reefs. Juvenile tropical inshore fish may be swept seasonally by the Agulhas Current as far south as the Cape of Good Hope, and the occasional great white shark may swim up from the south to visit the Protea Banks.

Mozambique's reefs remained untouched during the decades of civil war, but they are now open and sought-after dive destinations once again. Further north the islands of Comoros and Pemba have their aficionados. Their coral reefs exhibit good species diversity.

To the northeast, the volcanic islands of the Seychelles, with their striking granite formations, make for interesting diving. While the hard corals have been hard hit by the bleaching phenomenon of 1997–1999, the fish life is good and whale sharks visit the St Anne Marine National Park off Mahé Island in August and November every year.

In the far north, the Gulf of Aqaba and the Red Sea are more saline and warmer than one would expect from their geographical position. Volcanic activity at the sea floor increases the water temperature and the desert coastline does not have any large river systems flowing out. This has led to healthy reef development and good species diversity. Some 15 per cent of the species here, in the Arabian Gulf and the Gulf of Aden, are endemic as these bodies of water were cut off from the Indian Ocean when sea levels dropped in the last Ice

Age. Even when the ice melted and sea levels rose again, the sandy bottom and upwelling along the coast of Somalia limited the development of reefs and reef species, maintaining the isolation of the reef species to the north from the rest of the Indian Ocean.

The opening of the Suez Canal in 1869 resulted in heavy shipping traffic through the Red Sea, and as a result a profusion of wrecks now add interest to the diving here.

CENTRAL INDIAN OCEAN

The coast of Pakistan has low winter temperatures and most of the coast of India experiences massive seasonal outflows of fresh water laden with sediment from large river systems. Reef development under these conditions is very limited.

The islands off southern India – Lakshadweep, the Maldives, Sri Lanka and the Andaman Islands – have healthy reefs and good species diversity. Apart from Sri Lanka, these islands are remote, well clear of any mainland runoff. In Sri Lanka, most inshore reefs are damaged by blast and cyanide fishing, and divers should concentrate on the offshore reefs. The Maldives were severely hit by coral bleaching in 1997–1999, but the fish life remains exceptional and the reefs affected are already regenerating as they have done elsewhere throughout history. Divers will experience better diving offshore on live-aboard boats than at land-based resorts for the near future. The remote Chagos Archipelago has less species diversity, but again a quantity of endemic species.

EASTERN INDIAN OCEAN

Bangladesh and Myanmar (Burma) have massive seasonal outflows of fresh water laden with sediment, which limit reef development. The Andaman Sea, Southern Myanmar and West Thailand have topside landscapes dominated by huge granite boulders which make for wonderful underwater scenery, and some good diving off small reefs. Northwest Malaysia has a few reefs and good species diversity but, like the Straits of Malacca, suffers from agricultural runoff. The Straits of Malacca also have heavy shipping traffic, and as

this is a restricted water mass, the runoff lowers the salinity of the water in the Straits. However, the few small reefs have quite good species diversity.

Indonesia is at the centre of the richest coral and species diversity in the world, but blast and cyanide fishing are common and some islands have agricultural runoff. Those areas that have escaped the ravages of man have wonderful diving, however, and dive sites like Tulamben Bay off Bali offer a staggering variety of marine life.

The west and south coasts of Australia have some fine diving all the way round from the tropical northwest to the temperate south. Operators at Ningaloo Reef were the first to employ spotter-aircraft to locate whale sharks for their clients in the coral spawning season, and there is cage diving with great white sharks in the chilly waters around the seal colonies on the Neptune Islands.

ABOVE *A Napoleon wrasse* (Cheilinus undulatus).
RIGHT *A school of red-tailed, or collare, butterflyfish* (Chaetodon collare) *on a reef in the Maldives.*

WESTERN INDIAN OCEAN

SOUTHERN AFRICA

Stefania Lamberti, Judy Mann-Lang and Geoff Spiby

SOUTH AFRICA • MOZAMBIQUE • BASSAS DA INDIA

The great sweep of coast from Protea Banks off southern KwaZulu-Natal in South Africa up to the Bazaruto Archipelago off Mozambique provides a stunning variety of diving in warm, clear waters. This coastline offers adrenaline-charged diving with sharks, wreck and cave dives, a huge variety of game and reef fish, exciting night dives and great snorkelling.

Depths of dives vary from two to 60m (6.5 to 197ft), to the impenetrable depths off the sheer walls of Bassas da India in the Mozambique Channel.

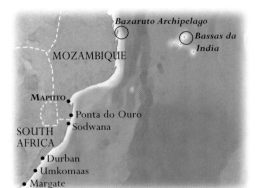

While there are good dive sites for seeing great white sharks further south, Protea Banks off the town of Margate is the place to go if you want to dive with large numbers of a variety of sharks in natural conditions. Every year in August the sardine run up the east coast of South Africa brings the sharks in its wake, and the grey nurse sharks (known locally as raggedtooth or sand tiger sharks) arrive at this deep and little-explored reef to feed and to breed. Later in the year thousands of game fish arrive, attracting a variety of sharks including bulls (known locally as Zambezi sharks), hammerheads and even the occasional great white.

The *Nebo* and the *Produce* provide interesting wreck diving at the Aliwal Shoal, but visibility is affected by river runoff and pollution from a nearby factory. The names of dive sites such as Raggie Cave and Shark Alley are testimony to the fact that this reef also provides excellent opportunities for diving with sharks.

Umkomaas, the little village where dive operators servicing the Aliwal Shoal are based, is a 40 minute drive south on the N2 highway from Durban. Margate is about a two-hour drive from Durban.

However, to visit South Africa's premier diving destination, Sodwana Bay, you must make a car journey of four-and-a-half to five hours north from Durban. The many coral reefs accessed via Jesser Point in this Bay are, uniquely, dominated by soft corals. They are host to a wealth of temperate and tropical fish and invertebrate species, whale sharks, rays, sharks, dolphins and turtles. A little further north, Mabibi Lagoon provides good snorkelling.

Long protected from over-exploitation by Mozambique's civil war, the reefs off Ponta do Ouro and the Bazaruto Archipelago now provide good diving on pristine reefs. With the return of stability to the country, Ponta do Ouro is developing into a popular dive resort. The islands of the Bazaruto Archipelago, once famous for their pearl beds, offer a paradisiacal getaway near reefs boasting healthy corals and many fish species. Whale sharks pass by, and visitors may even see dugongs.

Bassas da India is off-limits to most, but offers some exciting diving in a truly wild setting.

Previous pages Cousin Island in Seychelles.
Opposite Coastline typical of the northeast shores of South Africa and southern Mozambique.
Top right A boat being launched at Jesser Point, Sodwana Bay, South Africa's top dive destination.

CLIMATE
Subtropical in the south to tropical in northern Mozambique. Hot and humid in the summer months (December to March).

BEST TIME TO GO
Diving is good all year round. December/January can be very hot and humid.

GETTING THERE
International flights to Johannesburg (South Africa), and Maputo (Mozambique). Bassas da India can only be reached by yacht.

WATER TEMPERATURE
Averages 24°C (75°F).

VISIBILITY
It is generally good, but can be affected by industrial outflow at Aliwal Shoal.

QUALITY OF MARINE LIFE
Excellent, with many shark species, cetaceans including humpback whales and bottlenose dolphins, whale sharks and an abundance of game and reef fish, healthy corals and many turtles.

DEPTH OF DIVES
From shallow dives off Aliwal, Sodwana and Bazaruto to deep dives at Protea Banks, Cabo San Sebastian and Bassas da India.

SNORKELLING
Good at Sodwana, Mabibi, the Bazaruto Archipelago and Bassas da India.

PRACTICALITIES
It is advisable to take malaria precautions from Sodwana northwards.

SOUTH AFRICA

PROTEA BANKS

For years Protea Banks was exploited by deep-sea fishermen, and was a hunting ground for several daring South African spear-fishermen. It was one of these intrepid divers, Trevor Krull, who opened up the Banks to the world as a sport diving site.

Protea Banks is a long sandstone reef that runs parallel to KwaZulu-Natal's South Coast. It is about 10km (6 miles) long, extends for half a kilometre (0.3 miles) at its widest part and lies 8km (5 miles) out to sea from the holiday town of Margate. Its depth varies from 25 to 60m (80 to 200ft). Depth restraints have meant that this reef remains relatively unexplored.

Only a small area is regularly visited by divers, a stretch 4km (2.5 miles) in length and 200m (656ft) wide. This site starts at Northern Pinnacles – an area pitted with caves and overhangs. As the depth here starts at 30m (100ft) and reaches 40m (130ft), this is a dive reserved for experienced divers and a dive computer is useful.

Moving south from Northern Pinnacles, divers follow the inside ledge which connects the northern part of the reef to the southern part. Southern

Pinnacles has an average depth of 30m (100ft). The area's varied topography includes caves and gullies, each favoured by different types of fish, large and small.

Although Protea Banks is covered by a variety of dainty invertebrates that attract a number of different species of reef fish, this is not the reason for the Bank's reputation as a noteworthy dive site. Divers dare the deep reef to see sharks.

Protea Banks offers a different experience every season. The cooler counter currents that flow over the bank during the late winter months and early spring (August to November) bring the grey nurse sharks (known locally as raggedtooth sharks). These sharks congregate on the Banks as part of their mating ritual. They crowd the caves, gullies and overhangs, moving about sluggishly. With

mouths agape, and rows of large teeth protruding from their jaws, they allow divers to swim in their midst. At about the same time that the grey nurse sharks visit the Banks, the sardine run brings with it a following of hungry predators. Copper sharks leave their more temperate habitat to follow the abundant food supply. They are usually bottom-feeders, preying on slow-moving small fish, but during the month of August they obviously cannot ignore the surface frenzy of sardines.

ABOVE *Divers are treated to an exciting surf launch to get to Protea Banks.*
BELOW *Grey nurse sharks* (Eugomphodus taurus), *known locally as raggedtooth sharks, arrive at Protea Banks from August to November, to feed and breed.*

As the season changes and warmer waters wash over Protea Banks in October/November, the grey nurse sharks leave this reef and are replaced by thousands of game fish. Species include giant, blacktip, bigeye, bludger and yellow-dotted trevally; Cape amberjack; cobia; green jobfish; barracuda; sailfish; wahoo and eastern little tunny.

These are the fish that attract bull sharks and on occasion tiger sharks (the latter are most often seen from February to May). Both species have gained the reputation of being dangerous sharks, especially the bull shark. It is widely believed that this shark is responsible for many of the attacks on bathers and surfers along the South African coast, and yet, underwater they seem almost shy of divers, never venturing too close.

Hammerheads are regulars of the area. Schools of these strangely shaped creatures swim past over divers like squadrons of bomber aircraft on a mission. Hammerheads school throughout the year, but the best time to see them is in summer. Other sharks such as blacktip, mako and the occasional great white have no specific season.

At the completion of the seasonal cycle, different shark species will have come and gone, game fish will have crowded the waters over the Banks and the resident reef fish will continue their incessant quest for food. Stingrays will have skimmed the top of the reef and electric rays have been seen foraging in the sand.

Protea Banks has existed for centuries, unspoilt and unexplored. Now it has been offered to the world, not for its exploitation but for its protection.

ABOVE *A large potato grouper* (Epinephelus tukula) *and a juvenile golden pilot jack* (Gnathodon speciosus). RIGHT *Lyretail anthias* (Pseudanthias squamipinnis), *known locally as sea goldies, in among black coral at Protea Banks.*

ALIWAL SHOAL

Divers access the Aliwal Shoal from the small town of Umkomaas on the KwaZulu-Natal south coast, about 50km (30 miles) south of Durban. The reef, situated around 5km (3 miles) offshore, is about 4km (2.5 miles) long and 300m (980ft) wide, with depths ranging from five to 35m (16 to 115ft). The Shoal is dominated by a central ridge, an ancient sand dune that runs almost parallel to the coastline. This ridge is pitted with many caves and overhangs, shelves and gullies, all providing exciting glimpses of the colourful and varied marine life of the area.

Aliwal Shoal is the second most popular dive site in KwaZulu-Natal (after Sodwana), and an estimated 40,000 dives are recorded annually. A southern extension of Aliwal Shoal, Landers Reef, can be reached from a launch site at Rocky Bay, just south of the town of Scottburgh.

There is exciting wreck diving on the *Produce* and the *Nebo*, both close to Aliwal Shoal. The *Nebo*, which sank in March 1884 after hitting

the Shoal, is encrusted with *Tubastrea* cup corals and is home to enormous giant groupers. The *Produce* was wrecked on the Aliwal Pinnacles in 1974, and her crew rescued by local ski-boat skippers skillfully navigating heavy seas. This wreck is unstable and only suitable for experienced divers, but is also home to some very large giant groupers and some big moray eels.

Diving on Aliwal Shoal is certainly not for the faint-hearted. The surf launch from the mouth of the Mkomazi River and out to sea can be very tricky and requires an experienced skipper. However, once you have experienced the adrenaline-charged launch through the waves, you are ready for anything the shoal has to offer – from large numbers of grey nurse and bull sharks to giant, inquisitive potato groupers and dolphins.

Strong currents sometimes prevail, making drift dives preferable. A strong surge can make diving the caves and gullies of the Shoal dangerous. These are best explored on calm days. The minimum dive qualification is NAUI Open Water 1.

Aliwal Shoal is famous for the hundreds of grey nurse sharks (raggedtooth or sand tigers) that gather on the shoal. These sharks move northwards on a

ABOVE *Dive boats launch through the surf from the mouth of the Mkomazi River to reach Aliwal Shoal.*
BELOW *A myriad fish swim over the rugged coral-encrusted topography of the Shoal.*

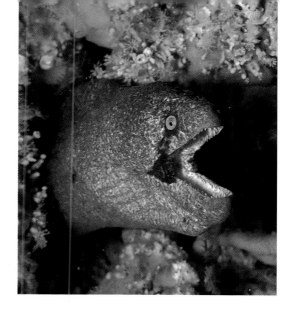

breeding migration and, between June and September every year, they gather on the shoal to mate, before moving north to Mozambique.

TOP *Black-cheeked moray eel* (Gymnothorax breedeni). CENTRE *A juvenile old woman angelfish* (Pomacanthus striatus). *It will change colour dramatically on maturing.* BELOW *The coral-encrusted wreck of the* Nebo.

Although grey nurse sharks look formidable, they are in fact rather docile and are only dangerous to humans when threatened. Their ragged teeth are adapted for grasping their prey of fish and squid, and they do not usually attack prey that they cannot swallow whole.

The reef is covered with a myriad colourful invertebrates and species of algae. Red algae and filter-feeding invertebrates dominate the shallow areas, while the deeper reefs are covered by brightly coloured soft corals and sponges. The kaleidoscope of colours of the invertebrates is matched by the wide range of colourful tropical and subtropical fish, such as the old woman angelfish, found on the shoal. More than 300 species of fish have thus far been identified in the area, and this includes a number of endemic species such as harlequin anthias (*Pseudanthias connelli*).

Large, fast-swimming game fish can sometimes be seen cruising along the shoal, while residential reef fish including groupers and sea bream are a common feature in some areas.

LANDERS REEF
Landers Reef, at a depth of 25 to 35m (80 to 115ft), provides more experienced divers with spectacular views of huge fields of pink thistle corals covering the reef, topped with a myriad of shoaling anthias. Large heads of smooth-horned hard coral (*Stylophora* sp.), a species only found off southern KwaZulu-Natal, are also abundant on the reef.

The Aliwal Shoal offers divers an exciting all-round dive. From the heart-stopping launch through the waves to regular sightings of sharks combined with beautiful reefs, interesting wrecks and hundreds of fish species – you are sure to return to shore on a diver's high.

SODWANA BAY

Sodwana Bay is situated on the Maputaland coast, 300km (186 miles) north of Durban. It is regarded as the premier dive site in South Africa, and more than 100,000 dives are logged at Sodwana Bay annually. The area forms part of the Greater St Lucia Wetland Park, a magnificent marine and terrestrial reserve controlled by the KwaZulu-Natal Nature Conservation Service.

A number of dive concessionaires operate from within the reserve, each with their own rustic dive camp. The reefs are reached by a relatively safe launch through the surf on fast boats powered by outboard motors.

The reefs at Sodwana Bay are clearly separated, running parallel to the shore and designated by their distance from the launch site at Jesser Point. Unlike most coral reefs, the Sodwana corals have grown on the remnants of ancient sand dunes which formed during periods of lower sea levels. Geologically speaking, the reefs are relatively young – only about 4000 years old. Another unique feature of the reefs is that they are domi-

nated by soft corals and not the hard corals found on most true coral reefs. A reason for the soft corals' success may be that they are less susceptible to damage by the powerful swells that move directly over the reefs during rough weather.

Sodwana Bay is in a subtropical transition zone between the tropics to the north and the warm temperate region to the south. This results in a great diversity of fish and invertebrate species. Hundreds of species of hard and soft corals, and sponges have been identified to date. However, as many invertebrates have not yet been intensively studied, new species probably await discovery. A large percentage of South Africa's coastal fish can be found in these waters and at least 25 shark and ray species and more than 400 bony fish have been identified.

The boat trip out to the reef may include sightings of whale sharks, dolphins or turtles, and possibly even a humpback whale further offshore. During a descent to the reef, huge shoals of snappers, goatfish and zebrafish may greet a diver. The concentrated variety of tropical reef fish found in

this area is quite unique and it is not unusual to identify as many as 50 different species on a single dive. This provides a treat for underwater photographers, especially as many of the fish appear to be quite unconcerned by the close proximity of divers.

The topography of the reefs is very varied, giving divers an opportunity to explore both flat areas

covered in soft corals and more dramatic rugged reefs with overhangs, gullies, caves and arches. Depths vary from nine to 35m (30 to 115ft). Some reefs are suitable for experienced divers only as they have large areas covered by fragile staghorn corals that are very susceptible to diver damage.

Under the right conditions, night dives in Sodwana Bay can be spectacular, introducing the diver to an exciting new world. Feeding corals, busy nocturnal fish seldom seen during daylight and sleeping sharks may all be observed.

The wide variety and pristine condition of both hard and soft corals, combined with the dramatic reef formation, the wide range of colourful reef fish and hundreds of different invertebrates make Sodwana Bay a unique and special dive site.

MABIBI LAGOON

There is excellent snorkelling to be had at Mabibi Lagoon, 25km (15 miles) north of Sodwana. Divers can see a variety of fish including juvenile angelfish, triggerfish, juvenile lionfish, butterflyfish, damselfish, blennies and surgeonfish. Invertebrates such as octopuses, nudibranchs, sea urchins and sea cucumbers may also be seen. Loggerhead and leatherback turtles nest in the vicinity.

OPPOSITE TOP *Jesser Point, at Sodwana Bay.*
OPPOSITE BOTTOM *A diver with blotcheye soldierfish* (Myripristis murdjan) *in Anton's Cave.*
TOP *An eyestripe surgeonfish* (Acanthurus dussumieri).
RIGHT *Soft corals and reef fish (mostly lyretail anthias, known locally as sea goldies) at Seven Mile Reef.*

MOZAMBIQUE

CLIMATE
Tropical; rainy season is November–April. Temperatures average 21–32°C (70–90°F).

BEST TIME TO GO
All year round, but December/January can be very hot and humid. Whale sharks are present in summer (September–May).

GETTING THERE
Direct flights to Maputo from Paris, Lisbon, Johannesburg and Harare. The best way to reach Ponta do Ouro is by four-wheel-drive vehicle from South Africa, via the Farazella (Ponta da Ouro) control post. The four main islands of the Bazaruto Archipelago all have airstrips with daily charter flights.

WATER TEMPERATURE
The average is 24°C (75°F).

VISIBILITY
Good but variable, affected by surge.

QUALITY OF MARINE LIFE
Abundant game and reef fish, and shark species. Whale sharks and dolphins are often seen. Bazaruto Archipelago is home to six species of turtle, and the shy dugong.

DEPTH OF DIVES
Average 25–40m (80–130ft).

SNORKELLING
Off Bazaruto Archipelago islands.

PRACTICALITIES
Take malaria precautions.

MOZAMBIQUE

From its southern border with South Africa at Ponta do Ouro up to its border with Tanzania in the north, Mozambique enjoys a great 2500km-long (1554-mile) sweep of coastline. However, for decades the country was shrouded in a cruel civil war and tourism dwindled in the face of ever-increasing violence. Once popular holiday resorts, abandoned by tourists, were raided by locals and became houses for refugees. The land was pillaged, yet the offshore reefs thrived, untouched and forgotten.

At the end of the war, with gunshots still echoing in the night, Mark Addison, an intrepid South African diver, ventured into Mozambique to the once idyllic coastal town of Ponta do Ouro. He was the first scuba diver to take the plunge onto these uncharted reefs. Several years have passed since his pioneering journey and today Ponta do Ouro and nearby Ponta Malongane are thriving resorts catering for sport fishermen, scuba divers and snorkellers.

The dive sites that Mark found are now world-renowned. Lining the coast, these vary in depth and topography – but the dive sites that stand out for uniqueness and quality of diving experience are Bass City and Pinnacles at Ponta do Ouro, and the reefs around the Bazaruto Archipelago – particularly at Cabo San Sebastian.

PONTA DO OURO

BASS CITY

Bass City, comprising five coral outcrops at a depth of 25m (80ft), is the domain of a stocky potato grouper (or bass) and his harem. This grouper, affectionately named Bert, has always welcomed divers. As you descend, Bert comes in for a closer look. Curious and quite nosy, he might single out a diver and try to bite gadgets such as torches, cameras and dive watches. Bert is followed about by a group of young golden pilot jacks who use the bulk of the large fish for protection. Occasionally, as the grouper hovers over sandy patches, they dart out and catch crustaceans and molluscs.

The five reef outcrops are covered in soft corals, sponges and algae that sway gently in the swell. Among them, moray eels take shelter in fissures. Thousands of sweepers and small-fry hover in dense clouds for protection, but they are easy prey for the fast-moving groupers that hurl themselves into the thicket, mouths agape. Where the reef meets the sandy floor lionfish lie motionless, waiting for unsuspecting prey to venture too close. Covered by a thin layer of sand, stingrays and electric rays wait for their chance to pounce. Marble electric rays are common here. Slow swimmers, they shock their prey with a jolt of current powerful enough to stun a human. Stingrays are faster moving, and eat animals that live buried in the sand. Their sting is for protection. While diving, look in every little hole to find the smaller creatures. Cleaner shrimps often accompany moray eels. They rely on the protection that the eels give them while attracting potential food close to the moray's mouth.

TOP LEFT *Mozambican fishermen at work.*
ABOVE *Bass City is known for large potato groupers* (Epinephelus tukula), *known locally as potato bass .*
CENTRE *Saddled butterflyfish* (Chaetodon falcula).
BELOW *Crown-of-thorns starfish* (Acanthaster planci).

PINNACLES

Pinnacles is quite far out to sea and a deeper dive, reaching depths of 40m (130ft). This a dive only for experienced scuba divers.

Although this reef is rich in corals, gorgonian sea fans, colourful schools of snappers and shimmering shoals of game fish, they are not the reason for diving here. Divers come to Pinnacles to see sharks; bull, silvertip and blacktip sharks patrol the depths. Silvertips and blacktips are pelagic swimmers rarely seen over reefs. In fact they are not well known sharks at all as they are difficult to follow, catch and study.

The depth makes for short dives and all too soon it is time to ascend – but the underwater pageant follows you to the surface. Schools of game fish come and go in the blue, the sharks may follow divers for a while, and for the lucky few a marlin may make a fleeting appearance.

On the way back to shore, the chances of finding whale sharks or a pod of dolphins are very good. The whale sharks hug the coastline on their migratory route in search of schools of plankton – their staple food. The dive boat stops and its occupants don masks and snorkels to swim with this gentle giant. Several pods of bottlenose dolphins are resident along this stretch of coastline. They have become used to the dive boats and allow snorkellers to swim among them.

ABOVE *A sea anemone and its attendant skunk clownfish* (Amphiprion akallopisos), *and threespot dascyllus, or dominos* (Dascyllus trimaculatus).

TOP RIGHT *Large forested sand dunes overlook the beach at Ponta do Ouro.*

RIGHT *A diver admires the ghostly spectacle of a large jellyfish drifting through the deep.*

BAZARUTO ARCHIPELAGO

The sands of Africa's east coast rise and fall beneath the shallows of the Indian Ocean, forming undulating, turquoise channels interspersed with sinuous islands. For early mariners these islands held promises of slaves, pearls and spices, but today, for the dive adventurer the offshore reefs hold a natural treasure rich in marine life.

The Bazaruto Archipelago lies halfway between Mozambique's two main cities, Maputo (the capital) and Beira. The five islands that make up this group – Santa Carolina (or Paradise Island), Bazaruto, Benguerra, Magaruque and tiny Bangué, were orphaned from the mainland some 30,000 years ago when rising sea levels filled the shallows between the African mainland and the sand dunes that had lined its shores. Beyond these shifting dunes, submerged sandbanks solidified into sandstone. Over time the tidal waters of the Indian Ocean carved an intricate maze of caves and gullies which formed the substructure of the archipelago's tropical reefs.

The archipelago's documented history begins in the 1700s when Phoenician and Portuguese mariners first discovered the pearl beds. The pearls are said to have charmed the Queen of Sheba, and to have been comparable in quality to those of Ceylon. Today these oyster beds provide food for coastal villagers.

It was, however, not just the oysters that made these islands an important stopover for ancient mariners. Tiny cowry shells were harvested by the locals and exchanged for goods with mariners. In turn the mariners used these as ballast and then traded them for silk and spices in the Orient. During this time cowry shells became a common unit of monetary exchange in the Indian Ocean.

The shallows between the islands are also home to pansy shells (or sand dollars), a relative of the sea urchin that is actually not a shell at all. These unusual, wafer-shaped creatures are covered in tiny spines that fall off when they die, revealing the dorsal 'pansy' pattern after which they are named. Sea-grass-filled lagoons are also home to the elusive dugong – a shy mammal seldom seen by visitors to the islands.

The natural attractions of the archipelago are not limited to offshore habitats, they extend from their shallow lagoons inland to freshwater lakes. For birdwatchers the islands are a paradise home to many species including frigate birds, falcons and migrants such as flamingos. There are a few species of endemic butterflies on the islands, and in the larger lakes there are freshwater crocodiles.

Twenty years of civil war safeguarded these islands from overdevelopment. In its prime Santa Carolina was a popular holiday and fishing destination. With the war the resort was abandoned and left to crumble into disrepair. Today the archipelago is still relatively untouched, with a lodge on Bazaruto, on Magaruque and two on Benguerra.

The reefs that lie parallel to the line of islands stretch from 20km (12 miles) north of Santa

ABOVE *Many of the islands in Mozambique's Bazaruto Archipelago enclose freshwater lakes.*
BELOW *Reef fish school for safety or when spawning.*

Carolina down to Cabo San Sebastian, a promontory south of the islands. All the reefs are easily accessible from the islands by yacht. The depth varies from just below the surface at high tide to more than 30m (100ft) at Cabo San Sebastian.

Great tidal movements between the open ocean and the shallows between the islands and the mainland can cause surge and varied visibility. As the tides flow in they bring with them clear water

---

ABOVE   *The region enjoys healthy corals.*
BELOW   *The Bazaruto Archipelago's reefs are rich in fish species, including anthias, groupers and butterflyfish.*

and huge schools of pelagic fish. When the tides flow out they carry with them churned up sand and nutrients, lowering the visibility considerably.

These pristine reefs are a showpiece for untouched marine environments. Situated between the Equatorial tropics and the South African subtropical zones, they have escaped the dangerous rise in temperature which has caused widespread bleaching on tropical reefs. Here hard corals produce a thriving community of coral polyps forming a rich carpet inhabited by a host of invertebrates and reef fish. Herbivores gorge on the abundant food sources while game fish come in from the deep to feed on reef fish.

The reef inhabitants include species found in no other ocean, such as the marbled coral grouper (*Plectropomus punctatus*) and the African butterflyfish (*Chaetodon dolosus*). The latter is rare even in the Indian Ocean. Schools of trevallies and barracuda make this a sought-after destination for anglers, whether they prefer deep-sea or flyfishing.

The caves and gullies of the reefs hide a variety of inhabitants. Juvenile reef fish swarm together within the dark interiors, hiding from predators and keeping out of the current. Nocturnal species rest up in the caves during the day and dart out at night to feed, and these include several shark

species. Whitetip reef sharks lie motionless under overhangs, having developed a way of breathing so that they do not have to swim to pass water over their gills. On the sand patches between reefs stingrays lie camouflaged, waiting for the right moment to dart out and catch their prey. Swimming just below the surface, whale sharks follow the coastline in their relentless quest for food.

CABO SAN SEBASTIAN

The most stunning of Bazaruto's dive sites is Cabo San Sebastian – a reef that can be located only with a GPS system. At first this spot was frequented by sport fishermen, who told larger-than-life stories of shoals of fish so huge that the waters boiled. When divers first ventured to Cabo they found the fishermen's tales to be true! Huge schools of game fish crowd the waters from the surface down to the reef, 30m (100ft) below. Potato groupers of more than a metre (3ft) in length protect their harems from predators, grey reef sharks patrol the edges of the reef, and huge turtles rest in caves.

Manta rays also visit the reef. They hover in the current, letting small cleaner wrasse go about their business. These graceful fish come in onto the reefs to be cleaned or to mate, offering scuba divers wonderful viewing opportunities.

BASSAS DA INDIA

Situated roughly halfway between Mozambique and Madagascar, this seamount thrusts up 3000m (9800ft) from the floor of the Mozambique Channel at around 11°S, 40°E. Few people have had the pleasure of visiting this site, which is uninhabited and can only be reached by private boat. The French Government control the site, and have declared it a marine sanctuary. A French gunship regularly patrols the site from its base on the island of Mayotte in the Comoros, and will see off anyone found exploring there.

The reefs consist of the slopes and the 100m-wide (330ft) rim of the submerged volcano, which has a diameter of around 11km (6.8 miles). This rim protrudes a metre (3.3ft) above the water at spring low tide, and encloses a lagoon that is 15m (50ft) deep at its deepest points. At high tide the flat, boulder-strewn reeftop disappears beneath the waves.

The real excitement of diving Bassas da India lies in the breathtaking wall dives. Gliding down over the gently sloping reef you pass over giant table corals at 15m (50ft), before reaching the edge of the drop-off at around 20m (65ft). Gripped by a mixture of apprehension and delight, you then drop over the wall, descending to 40m (130ft) before levelling out and allowing the current to carry you along the vertical wall. Schools of bluefin trevally materialize from the depths to take a look at you, and there is an enormous pink gorgonian sea fan enveloped in a cloud of pink anthias.

At 70m (230ft) – deeper than sport divers should dive – the wall disappears (it is actually undercut), and peering nervously out into the 'big blue' you can make out game fish like giant trevally and rainbow runners flitting through the gloom. On one dive, alerted by a yellowfin tuna swimming by at great speed, I looked down and saw a group of sharks approaching. Before I knew it three squadrons of around 15 hammerheads apiece were upon me. I was so amazed by their graceful synchronized swimming and close approaches (to within 4m, or 13ft) that in the 10 minutes that the sharks spent looking me over I didn't take a single photograph.

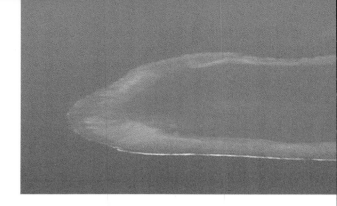

One of the pleasant aspects of diving Bassas da India is that you can complete your deep wall dives in shallower water, returning to explore coral outcrops spread across a sandy bottom in around 9m (30ft) of water. At this depth you can observe large schools of fusiliers, anthias and parrotfish, and solitary groupers, wrasse, butterflyfish and angelfish.

The Lagoon

There is only one way into the lagoon, via a shallow channel. Boats with a shallow draught can just about manage it at high tide. The lagoon makes a safe anchorage and the reeftop is littered with wrecks to explore. The most famous of these is the *Santiago*, a Portuguese East Indiaman that ran aground here en route to Goa in 1585. Salvage divers have recovered around 10,000 Spanish pieces of eight, emeralds, jewellery, 20 bronze cannons and a rare Portuguese nautical astrolabe from this wreck site. It took the members

---

LEFT *A diver passes a giant pink gorgonian sea fan.*
CENTRE *Whitespotted boxfish (*Ostracion meleagris*).*
BELOW *The top of the reef is littered with wrecks.*

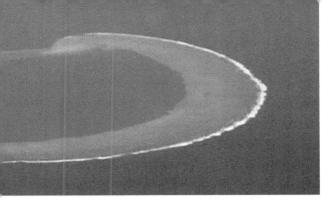

of our expedition some time to find the wreck, which we eventually identified by the 4.5m-long (15ft) anchor lying on the reeftop.

As a result of the great depth, it is best not to do more than two wall dives a day, and instead spend a lot of time snorkelling in between. Highlights of snorkelling here include swimming through huge schools of yellowtop fusiliers, and close encounters with giant trevallies – I saw three of around 50kg (110 lb) each.

Our expedition found a large area of dead corals covered in crown-of-thorns starfish (see page 51). It is commonly believed that these destructive starfish thrive where humans have disrupted the delicate balance of nature by removing their main enemy and predator, the triton shell. However, at Bassas da India this has not been the case, and tritons are present in abundance.

Although difficult to get to, Bassas da India must be one of the Indian Ocean's wildest and most beautiful dive sites. The great sunken volcano, encrusted with corals and the wrecks of numerous ships, is a pristine haven for marine life.

ABOVE *The rim of the submerged volcano is clearly visible in this overview of Bassas da India.*
RIGHT *Anchored on a narrow shelf outside the reeftop.*
BELOW *A thistle soft coral (*Dendronephthya sp.*).*

SOUTHWESTERN INDIAN OCEAN ISLANDS

Geoff Spiby, Lawson Wood and Judy Mann-Lang

COMOROS · SEYCHELLES · PEMBA ISLAND

These scattered island groups in the south western Indian Ocean have some fine dive sites in marine environments as yet relatively un-scathed by mass tourism. The region offers a wide range of dive types, from sensational wall dives in the Comoros islands and off Pemba Island, a vari-ety of wreck dives, great snorkelling throughout the region, exciting night dives, and the opportunity to dive with whale sharks in the Seychelles' St Anne Marine Park off the coast of Mahé Island.

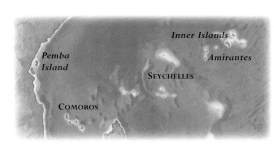

The four islands of the Comoros, or Perfume Islands, are situated at the northern end of the Mozambique Channel. Divers can enjoy a laid-back atmosphere with a variety of interesting shallow dives which are also good for night diving near the main island of the group, Grand Comoro.

The real attraction of these islands lies in the wall dives, the best of which lie some distance from the islands. The jewel in the crown of diving off the Comoros is undoubtedly Banc Vailheu, where divers can see a variety of sharks and large pelagic and reef fish in excellent visibility.

The far-flung island groups of the Seychelles offer some good diving. Believed to be a remnant of the great tearing apart of the continents that sep-arated Africa from India, their isolation has led to the development of interesting endemic animal and plant species, including the coco de mer nut. These islands have a distinctive and beautiful appearance, with white sand beaches and lush vegetation in among dramatic granite rock formations. Although not as rich in corals as the Red Sea, these islands more than make up for this by the great abundance in numbers and types of fish species found there.

The Inner Islands offer a good wreck dive on the *Ennerdale*, excellent day and night diving at L'ilot, and a deep dive at Shark Bank. You can snorkel at St Anne Marine Park, but more to the point for most visitors to the park, large numbers of whale sharks come here to feed in August and then again in November of every year.

The Amirantes, to the southwest of the Inner Seychelles group, also provides some excellent dives, including an exciting tunnel dive and the fish-rich waters around The Boulders.

Pemba Island, off Tanzania on the east coast of Africa, provides good diving on colourful reefs. Not many divers get to Pemba, and thus the corals are in good condition. Although the island has a fairly large resident population who fish the sur-rounding waters, fish diversity is still good and you will see large groupers, wrasse and tuna.

The visibility can be very good here, but is quite variable. The region is rich in coral and other invertebrate species – many of which have yet to be identified and counted. There are exciting wall dives and drift dives are popular in the strong currents. Night diving is also good, with a wide variety of nocturnal species.

Opposite The reefs off Pemba Island are rich in fish species including tangs, goatfish and butterflyfish.
Top right An unusual rock formation in Aldabra, Seychelles.

CLIMATE
Comoros and **Seychelles:** tropical, with a hot, rainy season from November–April.
Pemba: The rainy season is later here, the heaviest rains falling from March–July.

BEST TIME TO GO
Comoros April–November
Seychelles April–December
Pemba August–April or October–March

GETTING THERE
Comoros International flights to Hahaya International, on Grand Comoro Island.
Seychelles International flights to Victoria, on Mahé Island.
Pemba International flights to Nairobi (in Kenya) or Dar Es Salaam (in Tanzania).

WATER TEMPERATURE
Average 27°C (80.6°F)

QUALITY OF MARINE LIFE
Comoros You won't see huge schools of large reef fish due to bottom fishing, but there are vast numbers of smaller reef fish and invertebrates. Large pelagics are often encountered at Banc Vailheu. Hard corals at shallower depths have been hard hit by the bleaching caused by the El Niño phe-nomenon of 1997–1998.
Seychelles More than 900 species of fish, and the chance to see many large pelagics. Whale sharks visit St Anne Marine National Park in August and November. There is how-ever quite extensive hard coral bleaching.
Pemba There are a profusion of reef and pelagic fish, sharks including hammerheads, and invertebrate species. There has been coral bleaching in shallower water.

COMOROS

CLIMATE
Tropical, tempered by cool breezes. Hot and rainy from November–May; cooler and drier from June–October. The average land temperature is 25°C (77°F).

BEST TIME TO GO
April–November.

GETTING THERE
International flights to Hahaya International Airport on Grand Comoro Island.

WATER TEMPERATURE
Averages 27°C (80.6°F).

VISIBILITY
Varies from 15–40m (50–130ft).

QUALITY OF MARINE LIFE
Diverse and rich. Reef fish tend to be small due to constant fishing. Rare species include big longnose butterflyfish. There are plenty of pelagic fish, especially on wall dives, and numerous hard coral species and photogenic invertebrates.

DEPTH OF DIVES
Ranges from 10–40m (33–130ft).

SNORKELLING
Plenty of snorkelling reefs, but most only accessible by boat.

PRACTICALITIES
Proof of certification is necessary. Open Water 1 is fine for most dives, but Advanced Diver is necessary for Banc Vailheu. Antimalarial precautions are advisable.

COMOROS

Situated at the northern end of the Mozambique Channel, between the east coast of Africa and the northern tip of Madagascar, lies the Comoros Archipelago. It consists of four main islands – Grand Comoro, Moheli, Anjouan and Mayotte – and a few smaller islets, with a surface area of 2236km² (863 sq. miles).

The Arab sultans called the Comoros 'The Islands of the Moon' (due to the numerous small volcanic craters dotting the mountainsides), but today they are popularly referred to as the Perfume Islands because of the export of sweet-smelling perfumes from plants such as ylang-ylang and vanilla.

The islands are volcanic in origin, rising steeply from the ocean floor, their black fringing rocks in stark contrast to the lush green slopes of the mountains, the deep blue of the surrounding ocean and their long white beaches. The islands were originally occupied by Africans, then ruled by Arabs, the Portuguese and then the French.

In 1975 the Federal Islamic Republic of the Comoros was born, with Mayotte opting to remain under French rule. The Comorans are a blend of African, Arab, Malayo-Polynesian and Malagasy people, unified by the Islamic religion, dress and the Swahili language. Minareted mosques, narrow alleyways, old forts and dhow harbours proclaim a thousand years of Arab influence.

Mass tourism has not yet arrived in the Comoros, and most visitors base themselves on Grand Comoro (population 250,000), simply because that is where the international airport is, as are the best hotels and the only commercial dive operation. Island Ventures is a five-star PADI Gold Palm dive operation and offers more than 30 different boat dives, diver training including speciality courses, and the long range wall dives for which the Comoros islands are famous. This dive operation is situated at Le Galawa Beach Hotel at the northern end of Grand Comoro island. The island is 71km (44 miles) long and 34km (21 miles) wide, crowned by Mount Karthala, the world's largest active volcanic crater. The north crater is active all the time, though generally this is confined to vapour emissions. The last major lava flow was in 1972.

The first live coelacanth known to science was caught off the coast of East London, South Africa, in 1938. South African scientist JLB Smith described the new species and pointed out that coelacanths may be the ancestors of all land vertebrates. In 1952, a second coelacanth was caught off Anjouan Island in the Comoros. Since then more than 200 have been caught off Grand Comoro and Anjouan, and the Comoros is regarded as their true home. Specimens caught near South Africa, Mozambique and Madagascar are regarded as strays from the Comoros. Sensationally, a new species of living coelacanth was discovered off the coast of North Sulawesi Island in Indonesia in 1998.

Divers are unlikely to see coelacanths as they live at depths greater than 200m (656ft), unless they are lucky enough to see a fisherman haul one up from the deep. Preserved specimens are on display at the dive school and the National Museum in Grand Comoro.

COMOROS ISLANDS

Grand Comoro

Moroni

Moheli

Anjouan

Mayotte   Dzaoudzi

TOP LEFT *Comoran children play on traditional fishing boats, known as* galawas.

BELOW *A black-saddled toby* (Canthigaster valentini).

There are two types of diving in the Comoros. The first is on shallower, gently sloping reefs, mostly situated a short boat ride away from the dive school. These reefs consist mainly of hard corals, with gullies, cracks and overhangs. Here you will not see huge schools of oversized reef fish (as you would in the Maldives) due to the constant pressure of bottom fishing by the locals, but there are certainly vast numbers of smaller reef fish and plenty of the interesting reef creatures that divers enjoy. These include frogfish, stonefish, scorpionfish including leaf fish, lionfish, shrimps and a variety of nudibranchs. The hard corals are magnificent at greater depths (there has been some bleaching of corals at shallower depths), and areas of reef are carpeted in short, blue *xenid* corals.

The second type of diving is wall diving. There are a great variety of wall dives, but most entail a boat ride of an hour or two. Any of the 'denizens of the deep' can be seen on these dives, including giant tuna, sharks, manta rays, sailfish, marlin and whale sharks. Dolphins frequently escort the diveboats to these sites.

There is also the option of a 'sail-away' dive package to the uninhabited islets around Moheli, 92km (57 miles) south of Grand Comoro. The diving here is generally better and the marine life more prolific than that at Grand Comoro.

ABOVE *A juvenile* Ostracion cubicus *boxfish.*
RIGHT *Snorkelling off Moheli Island.*
BELOW AND BELOW RIGHT *Mushroom corals* (Fungia *sp.*).

MASIWA WRECK

This 74m (242ft) fishing trawler was sunk as an artificial reef in 1991 and lies just 10 minutes away from Grand Comoro by boat. It has an interesting history in that it was used by the infamous Bob Denard to smuggle 46 mercenaries into the Comoros in 1978 to successfully overthrow the Marxist government.

The wreck site lies between 12 and 35m (40 and 115ft). It is a superb wreck dive, which has attracted a variety of marine life. Large fish such as barracuda, tuna and bonito are often sighted here, and numerous lionfish and moray eels live in the wreck. A school of batfish hovers around the masts and will entertain you during your safety stop. Hard and soft corals are starting to colonize the wreck, as is a host of invertebrates. A certified wreck diver can do a penetration dive into her holds and superstructure, or this wreck can be used to do a wreck dive speciality course.

HAHAYA WALL

A 60-minute boat ride down the western side of the island will bring you to a true wall dive with the drop-off starting merely 10m (33ft) from the jagged volcanic rocks on the shore. Soft corals are rare, and the riot of colour comes from the prolific fish life. Angelfish, butterflyfish, parrotfish and schools of anthias abound. Gorgonians and amphora sponges dot the steeply sloping and at times sheer reef wall. Large game fish, especially tuna, are often spotted.

A safety stop can be enjoyed in the shallows on top of the wall, exploring for geometric morays, stonefish and other delights. The current is usually gentle and ideal for a drift dive.

BANC VAILHEU

This is undoubtedly the premier dive site of the Comoros. A 2.5-hour boat trip will bring you to this seamount 60km (32 nautical miles) from the Le Galawa Beach Hotel and 19km (12 miles) off the western shore of Grand Comoro. The seamount thrusts up from 2000m (6560ft) to a mere 10m (33ft) from the surface. The top is flat and the north and western edges form a sheer drop-off that extends for kilometres. From 10m (33ft) you drop down fairly steeply over the 'shoulder' of the reef, but from 20m (65ft) it becomes a vertical cliff dropping down to the distant ocean floor.

Visibility here is outstanding and you have the feeling of being suspended in midair as you are gently pulled along the wall by the current at a depth of 30m (100ft). Small, shallow caves with large trees of black coral punctuate the sheer drop. Giant dogtooth tuna, sharks, schools of rainbow runners and bluefin and giant trevally are often encountered, while mantas, whale sharks and hammerheads are also occasionally seen.

Moving up over the shoulder of the wall, from 20 to 10m (65 to 33ft), you find a coral garden of hard and soft corals with large shoals of fusiliers milling around, and clusters of brightly coloured anemones with their attendant clownfish. Huge honeycomb morays and stonefish add to this palette of colours.

The flat top of the reef is fairly barren and the safety stop is done by gently drifting along at a shallow depth, floating off the mount and watching sunbeams shafting down into the blue depths. This is a full-day, two-tank excursion.

BELOW *A* Sarcophyton trocheliophorum *soft coral.*
OPPOSITE *An anemone and its attendant skunk clownfish* (Amphiprion akallopisos) *at Banc Vailheu.*

SEYCHELLES
INNER ISLANDS

CLIMATE

The SE Monsoon blows from mid-May to the end of October, but the wind rarely exceeds 24kmph (15mph). The highest rainfall occurs around December/January, with the hottest months being March and April. Land temperatures average 27°C (80.6°F).

BEST TIME TO GO

April–November provide the most stable conditions. November is best for whale sharks. The Indian Ocean underwater film festival SUBIOS is also held in November.

GETTING THERE

International flights to the capital, Victoria, on Mahé Island.

VISIBILITY

Best from April–May.

QUALITY OF MARINE LIFE

Diverse, with more than 900 species of fish, including Whale Sharks, hundreds of invertebrates and corals. Some of the best night diving in the Indian Ocean.

DEPTH OF DIVES

The average is 18m (60ft), but the *Ennerdale* wreck and Shark Bank are deeper dives.

SNORKELLING

The Seychelles are probably best known for their snorkelling opportunities.

PRACTICALITIES

The local currency is Rupees, and US$ are preferable for exchange.

SEYCHELLES

Located in the heart of the Indian Ocean, the Seychelles are spread over a million km² (386,000 sq. miles) and comprise some 115 islands, in five main groups. The islands comprise two main geological types, granitic and coralline. Most of the inhabited islands are in the northeastern part of the archipelago. Here you will find Mahé, the largest island, as well as Praslin, La Digue, Silhouette and a few smaller granitic islands. These islands account for nearly 50 per cent of the Seychelles' landmass and are collectively known as the Inner Islands. Also part of the Inner Islands are Denis Island and Bird Island, both of which are true coral islands. The Outer Islands, by contrast, are all coralline. The coral atolls of Aldabra and Farquhar, the furthest from Mahé, each have 12 islands and the Amirantes group, to the southwest, around 25.

The Seychelles are remnants of the great divide in which Africa and India were separated in the Precambrian period, more than 650 million years ago. Like the Galapagos Islands, their volcanic nature, granite structure and oceanic isolation has resulted in the presence of a great many rare species of animals and plants.

Located north and northeast of Madagascar 1600km (1000 miles) from the African coast, the islands escaped human habitation until the early 18th century. Exotic and exciting, the Seychelles are a multiracial mix of Indian, European, Asian and African origins, all of which have created a culture as diverse as the marine inhabitants. The local language is Creole, a dialect with French, English and African roots.

First hailed as the Garden of Eden by General Gordon (of Khartoum fame), the subtropical Vallée

---

TOP LEFT *St Anne Marine National Park, from Mahé.*
OPPOSITE TOP *A beach on Mahé Island, showing the typical and striking granite rock formations.*
OPPOSITE BOTTOM *A grey reef shark (Carcharhinus amblyrhynchos) cruising a reef off Praslin Island.*

de Mai on Praslin Island hosts many ancient forest trees as well as a number of rare and exotic birds such as the black parrot. The 'forbidden fruit' – the coco de mer nut is only found in this valley. The nut strongly resembles the female pelvic region and its true origins were only discovered in 1881. It was thought originate from an underwater plant.

Visiting Praslin's sister island of La Digue is like stepping back in time with the only transport being by bicycle or ox-cart. The white sand beaches of La Digue are superb, with secluded coves sheltered by massive granite boulders amid swaying palm trees that jut out into the warm and clear waters. With the exception of exposed locations, there is little or no current around these islands, a lot of fish, a variety of colourful corals and an above-average chance of seeing large pelagics including manta rays, giant stingrays and the majestic whale shark. Apart from training dives from the shore, all of the diving is by boat and the majority of dive sites are just a 10- to 20-minute boat ride from the shore.

The Seychelles may not have the best coral reef dives as compared to the Red Sea, but it is the abundance of fish life that makes for great diving around these islands.

INNER ISLANDS

L'ILOT

To the north of Beau Vallon Bay at the exposed North Point of Mahé Island is the tiny granite outcrop of L'ilot. Comprising a tumble of granite boulders with a few lonely palm trees, the vertical walls and shaded boulders are festooned with marine life. An almost constant current passes through the narrow passage between the island and the shore, and this is responsible for the high concentration of marine life found here.

The southern wall is covered in *Tubastrea* cup coral and fringed with gorgonian sea fans and small stubby soft corals that fight for a hold in the current. In the more shaded areas of the sea

Praslin Island
Silhouette Island
Mahé Island
AMIRANTES ISLANDS
INNER ISLANDS
ALPHONSE ISLANDS
SEYCHELLES
FARQUHAR GROUP
ALDABRA GROUP

bed you are always able to find large anemones with their resident populations of skunk clownfish and, amid the boulders strewn offshore, there are huge numbers of small peppered moray eels surrounded by cleaner shrimps.

Only experienced divers are allowed to dive the site at night, because of the almost constant current, but it is then that you can find large numbers of Spanish dancer nudibranchs and their attendant symbiotic shrimps. This is an excellent dive and should not be missed.

ENNERDALE WRECK

The *Ennerdale* is a former British Royal Navy Fleet auxiliary motor tanker, owned by the Anglo-Norness Shipping Co. Ltd. Originally built by Lieler Howaldtswerke AG in Kiel in 1963, she was chartered to the Royal Navy in 1967. Weighing 29,189 tons, she was 216m (710ft) long x 30m wide (98.6ft wide) with a top speed of 15.5 knots.

The *Ennerdale*'s service with the Royal Navy Fleet lasted for only three years. On June 1st 1970, she sank on a sandbank after striking an uncharted rock, badly holing her starboard side. She went down 11.2km (7 miles) from Port Victoria at latitude 04°29'36"N, and longitude 55°31'22"E. She was loaded with 41,500 tons of refined furnace oil and gas oil to supply HM Frigate *Andromeda*,

when she ran aground. The *Ennerdale*'s 18 British officers and 42 seamen from the Seychelles all got off the ship safely. As it was judged to be a navigation hazard, the wreck was subsequently bombed and totally demolished by HM submarine *Cachalot*, after the oil slick had been cleared up by the Royal Navy.

The wreck now lies in three sections in 30m (100ft) of water. Dives tend to be around the stern section where the ship is mostly intact, with the wheelhouse and propeller readily accessible. The rest of the ship is largely broken up with the main part of the superstructure being quite open. The wreck is slowly undergoing colonization by small growths of soft and hard corals, with fire coral in abundance on some of the upper sections. As you descend to the ship, the water column soon becomes crowded with large schools of batfish that follow you for the duration of your dive.

The crumpled bows tend to have a congregation of stingrays and small whitetip reef sharks, but these soon head off into the blue as you approach them. The tangled superstructure is quite interesting, and as it is quite open, allows for relatively safe exploration. Due to the depth limitations of the wreck, it is better to swim back towards the stern, which is home to numerous moray eels, and where schools of batfish and orange-stripe emperors

vie for your attention. From here it is a safe and easy access up the mooring line to the dive boat.

SHARK BANK

Shark Bank is a series of massive granite pillars and boulders that sit atop a granite platform rising from 30m (100ft). Almost always subject to current, the rocky plateau is situated more than 8km (5 miles) northwest of Mahé. These pinnacles are a natural focus teeming with fish life not normally found nearer to the mainland. The walls are covered with bright orange sponges and white gorgonians. Large ribbontail rays are nearly always seen here. Big schools of batfish, small cowfish, hawkfish, snapper and grunt are found all over this rocky shoal, and you may see sharks. The depth of this site does impose time constraints and makes it unsuitable for trainees.

ST ANNE MARINE NATIONAL PARK

Just offshore from the capital, Victoria, lies the St Anne Marine National Park. The two largest islands within it are St Anne's (where the park rangers are based), and Cerf.

Some of the islands in the park are surrounded by shallow reefs, which are popular with snorkellers and day-trippers on glass-bottom boats. The main attraction to this area, however, is the chance to swim with whale sharks. Over many years, a large number of whale sharks have been sighted within the boundaries of the marine reserve. They come to feed on the plankton bloom which spirals up towards the islands from the southern Indian Ocean during August and then again in November. The latter is the best month for swimming with whale sharks.

Nothing quite prepares you for the massive rush of excitement and adrenaline as you slip into the water over the side of a boat and are faced with what can only be described as 'a monster of the deep'. When one is rushing towards you, mouth agape, with gigantic shark-like fins, your reasoning tells you that this shark is a plankton eater, but your instinctive, primeval reactions tell you that this is most definitely a shark and perhaps the scientists have got it wrong!

On a recent dive expedition to the park the excitement was palpable on our boat as we awaited instructions from the 'spotter' plane, a microlite buzzing overhead. Once word came over the radio, the dive boat was quickly moved into position ahead of the feeding whale sharks and we were then able to enter the water and approach the shark.

Sensing my puny presence in front of its wide, blunt nose, the shark veered to one side and looked me in the eye. The thrill of swimming with the largest fish in the sea is an unforgettable and humbling experience. We soon learned about the speed of these creatures as we tried to keep up with them. We saw the interaction of hundreds of remoras, cobia, juvenile golden trevally and thousands of jacks swarming around the whale sharks as they fed on the soup of stinging plankton and ctenophores (it is best to wear a full wet suit). The whale shark eats mostly plankton, that life-giving soup of the oceans. Very much a shark in shape, but reaching whale-like proportions, the fish has tough skin, gills, and a large vertical tail which it moves from side to side for propulsion. At 12 to 14m (40 to 46ft), it is the largest cold-blooded animal in the world.

Whale sharks are rarely seen any more than 500m (1650ft) from the shore as planktonic levels are highest in these areas. When approached by snorkellers and divers, the sharks often stop in midwater and 'stand' on their tails. When you come near them, it is important never to hold onto any of the fins or to try and ride them, as they will react as if being attacked from the rear. A 20-ton, 12m (40ft) fish which puts on a dangerous burst of speed is a formidable creature and can swat you aside like a tiny speck of flotsam.

ABOVE *St Anne Marine National Park has some good snorkelling but is best known for visiting whale sharks.* LEFT *Blue-yellow damselfish* (Pomacentrus caeruleus).

SOUTH FÉLICITÉ

This rather exposed site is located at the southern point of Félicité Island, east of the island of Praslin. Uninhabited and only accessible by boat, this lonely rock has peculiarly carved gullies and canyons shaped by tides and storms. These jagged outcrops spread, finger-like, out into water of a depth of 18m (60ft), and it is here that divers encounter large groups of sharks and turtles. It is not known why this site is such a focus for marine life, but whatever the attraction is, these creatures are found in large numbers on every dive. Nurse sharks can be found snoozing during the day and the sea floor is littered with pincushion starfish.

Although there is little current on this corner of the island, the area is subject to oceanic surge, which can make it difficult to get back onto the dive boat.

ABOVE *A snorkeller and accompanying fish are dwarfed by a whale shark* (Rhincodon typus) *in the St Anne Marine National Park.*
RIGHT *Clouds of anthias envelope a reef.*

SEYCHELLES
AMIRANTES ISLANDS

CLIMATE

As for the rest of the Seychelles.

GETTING THERE

Air Seychelles fly Monday, Wednesday, Friday and Sunday from Victoria on Mahé. The dive boat, *Indian Ocean Explorer*, also calls with divers on her regular trips down to Aldabra and the outer islands.

VISIBILITY

Best from March–June.

QUALITY OF MARINE LIFE

Even more diverse than the Inner Seychelles Islands, with a very wide range of most species found in the Indian Ocean.

DEPTH OF DIVES

Average depths are from 12–25m (40–80ft), but there are deeper dives off the edge of the shelf.

SNORKELLING

Excellent, as the surrounding lagoon is quite shallow and teeming with fish life. When conditions are perfect, it is exciting to snorkel over the deep holes and chimneys at the edge of the drop-off, where there are some amazing formations.

PRACTICALITIES

There is only one dive resort in the Amirantes, on Desroches island.

The nearest recompression chamber is located some distance away at the local hospital in Victoria on Mahé Island, in the Inner Islands.

THE AMIRANTES

The Amirantes or 'Admiral's Islands' are located around 320km (200 miles) southwest of Mahé and the Inner Islands, and comprise some 25 small islets, cays and atolls. Desroches is the largest in the group and has its own airstrip which services the Desroches Island Resort.

Well known to Persian traders long before Admiral Vasco da Gama first sighted them in 1502, the islands were once prolific producers of coconuts for copra production. Now the islands are barely inhabited, with Desroches being the most popular for that exclusive 'get away from it all' holiday.

Desroches Island forms the southern outer edge of a vast atoll that is largely submerged. The island itself is only a few metres above sea level and was once a thriving coconut plantation. The small village and landing stage has the remains of an old colonial-style house and copra equipment, and feral goats, sheep and chickens wander the streets. The resort on the other side of the island is quite luxurious and is near to the small grass airstrip.

It is a 15-minute boat ride from the resort to the edge of the wall, over a massive shallow lagoon where eagle rays and nurse sharks are often found. A few isolated coral heads are perfect for night

Banks
Africains

Rémire

D'Arros • St Joseph

Sand Cay • *Desroches*

Etoile • *Poivre*

Boudeuse •
• *Marie Louise*
Desnœufs •

AMIRANTES

ALPHONSE
GROUP

diving, but the best diving is undoubtedly on the edge of the wall. Here massive caves have been eroded into the limestone platform creating oases for shade-loving fish and corals. Huge red sea fans stretch out into the current and species not usually associated with the northern islands are found in abundance, including long-nose hawkfish, regal angelfish and three species of clownfish.

TUNNEL

From the beach at the resort's dive centre it is a 15-minute boat ride to the edge of the drop-off, where a mooring buoy has been attached to the old coral substrate. There is a large circular basin cut into the reef top here at 8m (27ft). The bottom of the depression is in 12m (40ft) and is cut by a long tunnel, which exits on the outer wall at 22m (73ft). There are always large schools of snapper and grunt sheltering inside this basin.

At the start of the tunnel you can usually find a sleeping nurse shark during the day, as well as a

TOP LEFT *An overview of Desroches Island, the largest in the Amirantes island group. It has a resort with dive facilities and an airstrip, so it is possible to fly to the island from Mahé.*
BELOW *Expanded* Dendrophyllia *coral polyps feeding.*

couple of giant moray eels attended by a variety of cleaner shrimps. The roof of the tunnel is covered in *Tubastrea* cup corals. Exiting the tunnel, you can turn either to the right or left and work your way along the edge of the deeply sculpted sides of the wall. Although appearing rather sparse in corals at first sight, the sea fans are all brilliant red in colour and the diversity of fish life is amazing.

THE BOULDERS

This site is around a 15 to 20 minute boat ride, in a more southeasterly direction from the shore entry, and is at the edge of the drop-off. There is a huge circular depression along the reef edge at a depth of 12 to 14m (40 to 47ft) with a tumble of boulders at the bottom. The maximum depth is 34m (116ft) on the outside of the wall, and the depth to the top of the boulders is 20m (66ft). In fact the entire length of this reef wall is cut by some amazing natural limestone formations with dramatic caves, tunnels and archways. Large red gorgonian sea fans stretch out into the current and the shaded areas are a mass of small, stubby corals and brilliantly coloured sponges.

As you enter the water, you are immediately engulfed by schools of Oriental sweetlips and Bengal snapper. All of the larger openings on the reef top form tunnels onto the outer reef. In the tunnels there are regular sightings of nurse sharks and numerous species of moray eels.

As you approach the outer reef wall, you are met by large stands of black coral and brilliant red sea fans, all of which have longnose hawkfish in residence, a species which is considered rare in the inner Seychelles group. Blue-spotted stingrays can be found on the reef top and under coral overhangs, and coral groupers lurk in the shadows waiting for unsuspecting prey to swim by. Solitary barracuda patrol the edge of the coral shelf and there are large bushes of black coral at the entrances to most of the caves.

ABOVE *A pink sea fan makes a stunning backdrop to a collection of reef fish including a cloud of lyretail anthias, or sea goldies* (Pseudanthias squamipinnis).
LEFT *A fan worm moves with the current in the seas off the Amirantes Islands.*

PEMBA ISLAND

CLIMATE
Tropical with hot summers (November to March). Heavy rainfall with a high humidity between March and July.

BEST TIME TO GO
August–April or October–March.

GETTING THERE
International flights to Nairobi (Kenya), or Dar Es Salaam (Tanzania). Flights to Pemba from Mombasa (Kenya), Zanzibar and Tanga (Tanzania). Ferry from Shimoni (Kenya), or Zanzibar and Tanga. Live-aboards depart from Mombasa.

WATER TEMPERATURE
Temperatures average 27°C (80.6°F).

VISIBILITY
Variable, but can be 20–50m (65–160ft).

QUALITY OF MARINE LIFE
Rich in species, many of which are yet to be identified and counted. The reefs are pristine with a profusion of invertebrate life, and both pelagic and reef fish.

DEPTH OF DIVES
From shallow dives to wall dives dropping off beyond the range of sport diving.

SNORKELLING
Pemba is excellent for snorkelling, but you should be aware of strong current action.

PRACTICALITIES
You will need a visa and a yellow-fever vaccination certificate.

PEMBA ISLAND

Pemba Island is situated 30km (18 miles) from the northeast tip of Tanzania, about 50km (30 miles) north of Zanzibar. The island is 60km (37 miles) long and about 20km (12 miles) wide, and diving is possible along the whole perimeter of the island. Diving around Pemba Island has concentrated on its western side, and there is the opportunity to discover exciting new reefs, especially on the eastern side of the island.

Although more than 250,000 people live on the island, it is still relatively undeveloped and most dives are conducted from live-aboard boats that operate from Kenya or Tanzania. A dive camp has recently been opened on the island, and it is possible to fly in to the airstrip at Chake Chake, or catch a ferry from Kenya or Tanzania.

Underwater visibility can be good, with 20 to 50m (65 to 160ft) not uncommon, but this is variable. Situated near the equator at around 4°S, water temperatures average 27°C (80.6°F). For divers looking beyond the more frequently dived sites of the Indian Ocean, Pemba offers an unrivalled opportunity to explore reefs that, to date, do not bear the scars of buoyancy-challenged divers crashing down on the coral.

Exciting wall dives are one of the main features of Pemba and the surrounding smaller islands. These dramatic dives take you from crystal clear shallow waters to sheer cliffs that drop off to more

than 200m (656ft). The walls are covered in hundreds of species of Indo-Pacific invertebrates, while the huge variety of fish species has yet to be counted. The area is a naturalist's paradise and many new species probably await discovery.

In shallower areas, sturdy, small corals abound. These species probably thrive here as they are more tolerant of the strong wave action. Colourful and delicate corals are common both here and on the outer reef slopes, and the contour corals, forming cascades down steep slopes, are particularly striking. At even greater depths, where light penetration is limited, there is an abundance of beautiful yellow sea fans and whip corals.

Emerald Reef at the southern extent of the island is covered in green-coloured corals, giving this reef a garden-like appearance. Large, pelagic fish are common near this reef, as are a wide variety of smaller, colourful tropical fish. A host of large groupers inhabit depths of up to 30m (100ft) here.

Fishing is common in the area and provides local people with much of their protein needs. However, despite this, the area still boasts huge

OPPOSITE LEFT *Pemba Island at sunset.*
OPPOSITE *A diver explores Pemba Crack.*
TOP RIGHT *Fishing boats ply the waters. The locals fish extensively, but fish diversity is still high.*
RIGHT *A bright red sea fan.*
BELOW *Small reef fish swim over an array of corals.*
FOLLOWING PAGES *Lyretail and yellowtail anthias (Pseudanthias squamipinnis and P. evansi) off Pemba.*

humphead wrasse, sweetlips, snapper, kingfish, barracuda and tuna. There are sharks, including hammerheads, and, of course, manta rays at Manta Point, where you can see as many as 15 huge rays on one dive (visibility is often poor, however).

Drift dives are the norm here, due to the strong currents. The wide array of nocturnal creatures makes a night dive off Pemba an unforgettable experience, and the area also offers good snorkelling. However, be careful of the strong currents.

The pristine condition of the corals at greater depths makes this a special place to dive. However, this brings with it the added responsibility of careful diving to ensure that the damage that has been inflicted on many frequently dived sites does not happen to the reefs off Pemba Island.

THE RED SEA

Jack Jackson and Lawson Wood

ISRAEL • EGYPT • THE SUDAN

The Red Sea fills the 1930km-long (1199-mile) depression along the faultline that separates the African and Indian tectonic plates at the northern extent of the Great Rift Valley. Long plied by Arab trading craft, it became a major thoroughfare for shipping when the Suez Canal opened in 1869.

A mere 350km (217 miles) across at its widest point, the Red Sea is linked to the Indian Ocean by a narrow inlet at Bab el Mandeb in the south. As a result it has almost no tides. The intense temperatures of the surrounding desert, the high levels of evaporation and the scant influx of fresh water as well as volcanic activity make it the world's saltiest sea. Volcanic activity heats the waters from the Sudan southward, to temperatures as warm as 30°C (86°F). The result is a rich ecosystem with more than 400 species of coral and almost as many fish and invertebrates as Australia's Great Barrier Reef. First made famous by divers Hans Hass and later Jacques Cousteau, the Red Sea can now be enjoyed by us all.

For many divers, the waters off northern Egypt *are* the Red Sea, and tourism here has expanded at an enormous rate. Twenty-five years ago, getting to the Sinai, Hurghada or Safaga was an expedition, and in those days it was easier to get to Port Sudan. A profusion of holiday resorts have since sprung up at Eilat in Israel, around Sharm El Sheikh, Hurghada and Safaga in Egypt, and more are being opened further south. As a result, local

airports have been set up to take direct charter flights and the intense competition has brought prices down to an all-time low. The explosion of dive tourism in the northern Red Sea has not been without its problems. In response to the damage done by boats anchoring directly on the reef, members of the diving community in Hurghada and Safaga formed the Hurghada Environmental Protection and Conservation Association (HEPCA) in 1992. Supported by USAID (the United States Agency for International Development) and the Egyptian Environmental Affairs Agency (EEAA), HEPCA was registered with the Red Sea Governorate and the Ministry of Social Affairs as a Non-Governmental Organization in 1995. The association installs and maintains fixed mooring buoys, trains the boating and diving community and cleans up the beaches and the islands. HEPCA's operations extend south to The Brothers Islands, Dædalus Reef, Gezîret Zabargad and Rocky Islet.

In contrast, the Sudan has suffered a decline. Divers must persevere to get there. Live-aboard boats continue operating out of Port Sudan and carriers fly to Khartoum, but the customs here can be a problem when it comes to camera or video equipment, and the flights to Port Sudan are unreliable. Nevertheless, it is well worth making the effort, with some stunning diving at Sha'b Rumi, Sanganeb, and on the *Umbria* wreck.

Opposite Elphinstone Reef.
Top right A diver peers through a porthole on the *Thistlegorm* wreck.

DIVING THE RED SEA

DEPTH OF DIVES

Dives of 30–40m (100–130ft) are common for experienced divers, but 25m (80ft) is deep enough to see most things of interest. Remember that the only working hyperbaric chamber is at Sharm El Sheikh, so dive conservatively.

SNORKELLING

Be wary of points with currents where sharks are found – they may mistake a snorkeller on the surface for a fish in trouble and attack them.

BUOYANCY

Do a buoyancy check when you arrive if you are not accustomed to diving in this extremely salty water.

PROTECTIVE CLOTHING

This is necessary as protection against fire coral and stinging hydroids. At night lionfish are also a problem.

EAR INFECTIONS

These are common with both divers and snorkellers, and are usually caused by fungus. It is advisable to use an ear-drying agent after each dive.

EQUIPMENT

In the Sinai and south Egypt dive operators stock a limited range of equipment and divers should ideally be self-sufficient, carrying their own dive equipment and spares, prescription medicines, decongestants, batteries and film. There is no equipment on sale in the Sudan.

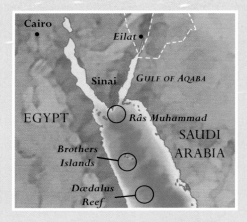

ISRAEL AND EGYPT

CLIMATE

Eilat and **Sinai:** warm and dry in winter, average temperature 20°C (68°F); hot and dry in summer, average 35°C (95°F). Off Sinai the wind can be strong in winter so take warm clothes. **The Brothers**, **Dædalus** and **Elphinstone:** pleasant temperatures in summer as a result of the offshore winds.

BEST TIME TO GO

Eilat and **Sinai:** May–September.
The Brothers and **Dædalus:** May–July.
Elphinstone: April–September.

GETTING THERE

Eilat: charter flights land at Ovda military airport, 40 minutes away by road. **Sharm El Sheikh:** direct charter flights to Sharm El Sheikh airport, or connecting flights via Cairo; 15 minutes away by road. **Hurghada:** charter or connecting flights via Cairo to Hurghada airport.

WATER TEMPERATURE

Eilat and **Sinai:** summer average 25°C (77°F), winter 19°C (66°F). **The Brothers, Elphinstone** and **Dædalus:** summer average 27°C (81°F).

VISIBILITY

Eilat averages 12m (40ft) due to shipping. Elsewhere expect at least 20m (65ft), and 30–40m (100–130ft) over deep water.

QUALITY OF MARINE LIFE

Sinai and south Egypt have a high density of stony and soft corals, gorgonians, other invertebrates and both reef and pelagic fish.

ISRAEL AND EGYPT

DOLPHIN REEF

Although dolphins seem to always be ready to enjoy riding the pressure wave ahead of fast moving boats, encounters between divers or swimmers and dolphins in the water are rare. Worldwide there have been several instances of lone male bottlenose dolphins (*Tursiops truncatus*) making wilful contact with swimmers, and some resorts in the Caribbean have encouraged dolphins to interact with humans. A similar facility has been set up at 'Dolphin Reef', next to the port of Eilat at the northern extent of the Gulf of Aqaba.

A large area of sea, averaging 12m (40ft) deep and enclosed with buoyed nets, is home to a group of bottlenose dolphins rescued from Russia and Japan. Despite their different geographic origins, they seem to be quite happy living as one boisterous group, a point proven by the fact that many of the females have calved. The dolphins can jump the net to freedom and some do, usually returning some time later with fresh propeller scars on their backs. The enclosure also contains many reef fish, moray eels, cobia, and some very large, habituated stingrays. Sea lions from a smaller netted enclosure beside the dolphin enclosure regularly jump the net to join in the fun with the dolphins, divers and snorkellers.

Many experts have commented on an uplifting effect experienced by patients suffering from depression and mental illness when swimming with dolphins, so Dolphin Reef is fully equipped to deal with swimmers who have special needs, including the blind and those normally confined to wheelchairs. A member of the staff must accompany all participants. Snorkellers enter the enclosure over the net, but divers enter through a sliding curtain at the bottom. The dolphins are sensitive to the noise of this curtain being opened and immediately appear, energetically passing by at high speed with lots of clicking and shrieking. Do not expect them to pose – once they have had a quick inspection of the newcomers and searched the accompanying regular staff for titbits of food they go back to their boisterous play, occasionally preying on reef fish and not at all shy about copulating in front of *Homo sapiens*.

During the day the dolphins see hundreds of divers, so they could be forgiven for becoming bored with them; it is best to book the first dive of the day, before the sand gets stirred up and when the dolphins have not had human contact overnight so that they are likely to be more curious.

The dolphins and stingrays are fed from rafts above water, and handfed in the water – though the resulting churned-up sand makes the visibility even worse. Much has been said against keeping marine mammals in oceanariums, but these animals are free to leave if they wish to. It is debatable whether they could survive in the wild on their own after a life in full captivity, but in the meantime here is a chance to see live dolphins close up and for children in particular this is an effective way to pass on the message of conservation.

ABOVE *The aquarium and underwater observatory at Dolphin Reef, Eilat.*
BELOW *Feeding a bottlenose dolphin from a raft.*
OPPOSITE *Divers can interact with the dolphins.*

BOTTLENOSE DOLPHINS

Dolphins are are essentially small, toothed whales and like us are warm-blooded, air-breathing mammals, giving birth to live young. Most true dolphins have a beak and a prominent dorsal fin. The bottlenose dolphin (Tursiops truncatus) can reach 4.2m (14ft) and weigh over 650kg (1330 lb). All dolphin teeth are the same — there are no molars or incisors and they are sharp and peg-like in shape for catching prey. Dolphin ages can be judged by counting the growth rings in their teeth, as with a tree.

Dolphins differ from porpoises in that they have a beak whereas porpoises have a rounded head, and they have a larger dorsal fin. Porpoises have teeth that are flattened in cross-section.

Probably the best known cetacean because of its widespread use in marine parks and research facilities, the bottlenose dolphin has a short and stubby beak — hence the name 'bottlenose' — and a more flexible neck than other dolphins. There is considerable variation in their colour, but generally they are light grey to slate grey on

the upper part of the body, countershaded to lighter sides and pale, pinkish grey on the belly. The belly and lower sides are sometimes spotted. Individuals in the Indian Ocean are often darker than those in the Pacific. The curved dorsal fin is located near the middle of the back and males are larger than females.

Bottlenose dolphins are found worldwide in temperate and tropical waters, and are often encountered in harbours, bays, lagoons, estuaries, and river mouths. There are two subspecies; the more predominate coastal form, and the smaller offshore form. There is evidence that the offshore populations in temperate waters migrate towards the equator in autumn and return to their richer feeding grounds in the spring. Social groups of bottlenose dolphins are called a pod. These are usually smaller than 15 individuals, but groups of more than 1000 have been seen. They often shoal with pilot whales.

Inshore bottlenose dolphins eat a variety of fish and squid and will often work together to herd shoaling fish into a tight ball — and then take turns to charge into

the shoal to feed. In some areas dolphins herd fish into shallow water — or onto mud or sand banks, where the dolphins will actually beach themselves temporarily — to catch them. Offshore bottlenose dolphins can dive to more than 600m (1970ft) to catch bottom-dwelling fish.

They live for 25 to 30 years, males reaching sexual maturity at about 11 years, and females at five to seven years. Bottlenose dolphins are sexually active throughout the year, but females are fertile only during spring and summer. Their gestation period is 12 months. 'Nurse' dolphins often help newborn calves to the surface to take their first breath.

A dolphin uses echo-location to find prey in dark or murky water. A series of 'clicks' are emitted through its forehead and the echoes heard through its jaw enable the animal to form images of prey, even if the prey is buried under the sand. Dolphins also have personal signature whistles that they use to communicate with one another.

RÂS MUHAMMAD MARINE NATIONAL PARK

Created in 1983, this fabled marine park is located at the southern tip of the Sinai Peninsula and geographically separates the Gulf of Suez to the west and the Gulf of Aqaba to the east. When the park was first opened it only covered Râs Muhammad's immediate environs as well as Tiran and Sanafir islands. It now covers from the Sha'b Mahmûd reefs to the west, the Strait of Tiran, past Râs Nasrani to Râs Abu Galum, which is almost halfway along the east coast of the peninsula, towards Israel.

Formed over millenia, this coralline limestone headland dominates the coastline and includes the world's most northerly mangrove forest, sheer vertical walls that drop thousands of metres, submarine peaks and a wide selection of dives in a variety of habitats. The reefs and walls are best known for the large variety of hard corals, rainbow-hued soft corals, colourful basslets and clouds of anthias. Huge Napoleon (humphead) wrasse vie for your attention amid schools of batfish and snapper. Large moray eels are common, as are scorpionfish and the dreaded stonefish.

Populated by the Bedouin tribes, the southern Sinai has very hot dry summers, virtually no humidity and minimal rainfall. Freezing temperatures in the winter desert contrast with often semi-tropical water temperatures. The contrast between the bleak, lunar landscape and the majestic reefs with their colourful corals and teeming marine life of every hue and shape is quite staggering, and keeps divers returning year after year.

Underwater visibility is generally better than 30m (100ft), but like all of the world's seas is subject to seasonal fluctuations. Spring and autumn plankton blooms cloud the visibility for brief periods. Water temperatures range from 28°C (82°F) in summer to the lower 20s celsius (70s°F) in winter.

Although there is little tidal movement – only a one metre (3ft) change during the equinox – as a result of its geographical position at the vortex of three major waterways, Râs Muhammad can be subject to severe underwater currents. Divers should therefore take every precaution when visiting the fabulous walls of the park.

Most of the diving in the area is done from the day-dive boats, which make the two-hour trip from Sharm el Sheikh with groups of up to 20 divers per boat. Divers will do two dives on the undersea islands within the park, and lunch is included. There is an entry fee to the park and all foreign nationals must hand

---

TOP *An aerial view of Râs Muhammad.*

LEFT *A* Gyrostoma helianthus *anemone.*

ABOVE CENTRE *A juvenile Napoleon wrasse (*Cheilinus undulatus*). In this region they are quite approachable.*

OPPOSITE *A reef dominated by fire and stony corals.*

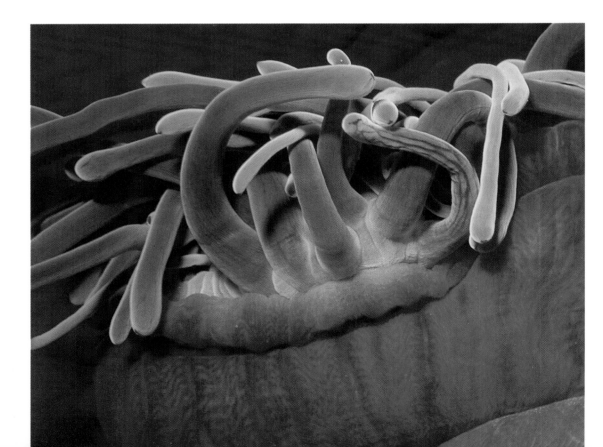

over their passport to the dive shops for their details to be recorded. The area can get crowded, and with only a couple of permanent moorings, most dive boats join onto one another to form a floating pontoon while diving is taking place.

Râs Za'atar

Although classified as being located in the Râs Muhammad Marine Park, Râs Za'atar is the last reef corner before the massive fjord-like inlet known as Marsa Bareika. This very exposed headland is best dived in the morning when the sun shines down into the depths of the reef, highlighting the large soft corals (*Dendronephthya* spp.).

There are massive undercut canyons along this vertical wall, which plunges way below safe diving depths. As you approach the corner, the current generally picks up and the narrow caves near the surface are home to thousands of glassfish, stalked by lionfish and large squirrelfish.

Around the corner, in sheltered Marsa Bareika, the shallows are home to hundreds of masked pufferfish. There are several large caverns here, which are framed in soft corals and black coral trees, and absolutely filled with fish.

FACT FILE ON THE RED SEA

No one is sure how the Red Sea, El Bar Ahmer in Arabic, came to be called red. It could be due to the sunsets, sandstorms or the 'red tides' of plankton that sometimes occur; however all of these are common to other tropical seas. Some authors hypothesize that because the Arabic name for the Mediterranean, El Bar Abyad (the White Sea), is derived from the white limestone cliffs along its shores, the Red Sea must be named after the light scattered through the sand and dust of the desert coastline.

Although the Red Sea extends from the Gulf of Suez in the north to the Bab el Mandeb (the Gate of Tears) in the south, there are various reasons as to why only the northern half is popular with divers. The main incentive is cost; charter flights and the competition between many operators have made Eilat in Israel, Aqaba in Jordan, and all of Egypt very good value, while the Sudan is not far behind.

Since the completion of the Suez Canal in 1869, all of the Red Sea is a busy shipping lane. It becomes more crowded where it narrows in the Gulf of Suez, and there are active oilfields here, so no sport diving occurs from just north of the Straits of Gûbal.

Saudi Arabia has several areas that offer good diving though some areas near to ports have suffered from spear-fishing by Far Eastern guest workers. It is only very recently that Saudi Arabia has allowed tourists in, but so far this has not included divers, and sport diving here is limited to those with work permits. Some people have managed a few dives while travelling through on transit visas.

Before the Ethiopian War Eritrea was known for its diving, but generally has poor visibility. Eritrea has gone to war with Ethiopia, and more importantly for divers, has seized Yemen's best diving island, Hanish Kebir. The World Court has found in favour of Yemen over the legal rights to this island but at present boats approaching the Hanish Islands are shot at. Yemen has good diving and was be-coming popular with divers,

but the Eritrean problem together with recent deaths of tourists has eliminated tourist interest.

Highly saline, the Red Sea is the result of the landmasses of Africa and Europe separating at 1.27cm (0.5 inches) a year. Renowned for its water clarity, reef-building corals living in symbiosis with zooxanthellae extend deeper than in most other coral seas. The land adjacent to the Red Sea is generally mountainous with a low, sandy plain to the shore. In Egypt there is very little rain or cultivation and no rivers flow into the Red Sea from here.

The Red Sea is one of the deepest seas in the world, reaching 3040m (9970ft) between Port Sudan and Jiddah. Here hot brine pools have been measured at 60°C (140°F), suggesting that the brine is over 100°C (212°F) when it is extruded. The Red Sea also has a number of rocky islets together with coral reefs that come to within 0.6m (2ft) of the surface. In summer, when the sea level is at its lowest, parts of these reefs may break the surface.

When European divers first discovered the delights of diving in the northern Red Sea it was all shore or near-shore day-boat diving. Quite hot in summer, Eilat, the Sinai coast and the coast south of Hurghada gained popularity as winter destinations. However the offshore diving can be quite windy so it is more comfortable in summer.

The junction of the Strait of Gûbal with the Strait of Tiran often has tricky winds and currents so the area is a haven for divers who delight in shipwrecks. The Strait of Tiran is particularly busy with divers so the area is limited to day-boats. Live-aboard boats are requested not to dive here.

RÂS MUHAMMAD

Râs Muhammad, at the tip of the Sinai Peninsula, is perhaps the most famous dive site in the National Marine Park, with some truly magical dives from depths of just a few centimetres below the surface to the maximum depths to which sport divers can safely dive.

Largely undercut in many places, the dive known as Shark Reef is a true paradise, not only for divers, but also for large numbers of schooling fish, particularly during the summer months when batfish, barracuda, emperorfish and jacks form massive schools. The wall at Shark Reef is covered in brilliantly coloured soft corals and large gorgonian sea fans are found on the deeper slopes.

The second submerged reef is now known as the Jolanda Reef, after the ship that ran aground here, spilling her cargo of toilet bowls and sinks, containers of pet food, a BMW car, gas pipes and cement. She finally slipped over the edge of the continental shelf during a violent storm in 1987,

ABOVE *The point at Râs Muhammad, at the southern tip of the Sinai, bathed in warm evening light.*
LEFT *The Strait of Tiran is littered with shipwrecks. Visible here are (from front to back); Gordon, Thomas, Woodhouse and Jackson reefs. To the left side of Gordon Reef, as pictured here, there is a light beacon. It was set up to prevent ships from running aground on the reef, as did the large commercial freighter visible here. Of these four reefs, Jackson and Thomas reefs are the better ones to dive.*

leaving behind her trash in the valley between the reef and the mainland.

Crocodilefish are common here, as are lionfish, and the deadly stonefish can also be found in the shallows. Better known for the sheer majesty of the vertical walls and the purple soft corals (*Dendronephthya klunzingeri*), the area actually has three submerged island reefs, the remains of the shipwreck *Jolanda* and a massive plateau near the shore where literally hundreds of anemones and their clownfish partners can be found. Nowhere else in the northern Red Sea can such large numbers of both species be found.

Divers exploring the site should beware, however, as the area is guarded by a very large titan triggerfish. This aggressive fish is very territorial and will attack divers who unwittingly stray into its home patch. It protects its nesting area with a very sharp set of teeth, which have been known to cut through a diver's fins.

Across the natural amphitheatre you can just make out the start of the Râs Muhammad wall and seemingly bottomless depths extending for thousands of metres below. Largely undercut, the wall is a moving mass of anthias and fairy basslets, which light up the sea ahead of you as you drift round in the almost perpetual current.

Near the saddle between the two islands there are large schools of batfish and spangled emperorfish. The walls here support massive gorgonian sea fans, all of which appear to have their own resident longnose hawkfish.

CROWN-OF-THORNS STARFISH

The crown-of-thorns starfish (Acanthaster planci) gained notoriety in the 1960s and 1970s when population explosions caused massive coral reef destruction in the Indo-Pacific. Some blamed the depletion of its natural predators such as tritons, pufferfish and triggerfish. Others pointed out that many of the worst hit areas were those affected by blast fishing, harbour construction, dredging and pollution, with consequent removal of the smaller creatures and some corals that eat Acanthaster planci at the egg and larval stage. A female can produce 12 to 24 million eggs each year.

Some crown-of-thorns explosions seem to be related to periods of heavy rainfall runoff, or runoff from logging or intensive agriculture, particularly where the natural barrier of mangroves has been destroyed. The more nutrient-rich runoff leads to an increase in the phytoplankton on which the starfish larvae feed. However, core samples drilled through the Great Barrier Reef suggest that these population explosions have occurred regularly throughout history and it may just be that with scuba diving becoming popular, there are many more divers and marine scientists in the water to observe them.

Around 30cm (12in) across, with up to 23 arms — which are covered with short fat spines, three to 5cm (0.8 to 2in) long on the dorsal surface — Acanthaster planci varies in colour from grey through orange to purple. The starfish feeds on live coral polyps, preferably those of Acropora table corals, by lowering its stomach over the coral so that its digestive enzymes come into direct contact with

the coral tissue. Thus digestion has already begun before the food has been taken into the mouth. These enzymes may also cause the severe skin reaction suffered by divers who pick them up without gloves.

Acanthaster planci regularly return to the same coral table until that table is completely dead. When aggregations occur, newcomers are attracted to the coral that is already being eaten by existing starfish, so it is likely that the chemicals given off during feeding attract other starfish.

Normally Acanthaster planci feed at night, preferring to hide deep in crevices during the day. Aggregations occur naturally, possibly associated with breeding or feeding activities. Where these occur, many individuals make less effort to hide during the day, often only crawling beneath a coral table in the shade. Others can be seen moving through shady areas towards their prey, an hour or so before dusk.

Many attempts have been made to eradicate these starfish when their populations explode, but none have been fully effective. Damaged starfish can regenerate and the chemical injections which do finish them off are expensive, slow and inefficient. The only sure solution is to collect them up, bring them ashore and bury or burn them.

LEFT *Tritons eat crown-of-thorns starfish.*
BELOW *The destructive crown-of-thorns starfish (Acanthaster planci). Population explosions of these starfish have decimated corals in parts of the Indo-Pacific region.*

THISTLEGORM WRECK

The 4898-ton, 126.5m-long (415ft), 365-horse-power *Thistlegorm* was built by JL Thompson & Sons at Sunderland in 1940. Requisitioned and armed by the Navy, she set off with supplies for the 8th Army at Alexandria in North Africa. Because the Germans and Italians had control of

most of the Mediterranean she sailed the long way, around the Cape of Good Hope, and was escorted up the Red Sea to Suez.

Laden with military equipment – from vehicle and aircraft parts, motorcycles, gun carriers, munitions and railway locomotives to radios and Wellington Boots – she was waiting with other ships at Sha'b Ali for clearance to enter the Suez Canal when two German Heinkel bombers from Crete found and bombed them.

Early on October 6th 1941 two bombs hit the aft holds containing the ordinance. The resulting explosions ripped a huge hole in the aft section and set the ship on fire. Nine of the crew were killed, and, as was the custom at the time, the surviving crew's pay was stopped and they had to make their own way home. This wreck was marked on early postwar charts as a danger to

shipping, and in the early 1950s it was easy for Captain Jacques Cousteau and his crew to find her and salvage some artifacts (including the Captain's safe). They filmed and wrote about the wreck; both the film and the book were called *The Living Sea*. What is surprising is that despite the fact that the surrounding area had subsequently been much dived, everyone except the local fishermen forgot about the wreck

In early 1990, divers woke up to the fact that she was out there, began asking questions and soon rediscovered her. Not as good as the *Umbria* wreck because the visibility was often poor and the currents strong, in those days she was reminiscent of a war museum. Tool kits could be found under the seats of the motorcycles, nurse sharks and huge groupers rested among the wreckage and the handrails were covered in corals and sponges. Despite attempts to keep the discovery quiet, word soon got out and the divers arrived in hordes. Among them were the wreckers.

Today, the *Thistlegorm* resembles an underwater army surplus store to the northeast of Shag Rock, east of the southern end of Sha'b Ali, northwest of Râs Muhammad. She lies almost upright, slightly listing to port except for the stern section, which lies heavily to port. The bottom of the bow is at 30m (100ft), the propeller and rudder are at 32m (105ft), the superstructure rises to 12m (40ft) and the locomotives were thrown to either side.

Conditions vary, but if you get there early she is still a tremendous dive. The holds contain an assortment of the implements of war, and the hull is a substrate to stony and soft corals, sponges and most species of Red Sea reef fish.

OPPOSITE TOP *Goatfish* (Parupeneus *sp.*) *swim past the coral-covered railings on the* Thistlegorm *wreck.*
OPPOSITE BOTTOM *A longsnout flathead crocodilefish* (Thysanophrys chiltonae).
BELOW *The hold of the wreck still contains military equipment, including this motorcycle.*
RIGHT *Exploring the* Thistlegorm *wreck.*

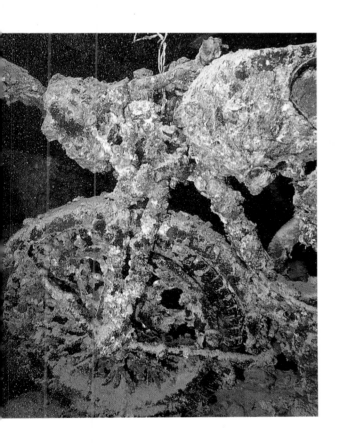

SHA'B 'ABU NUHÂS

Midway between the Sinai Peninsula and the Egyptian mainland lies a small submerged reef, just north of Shadwan Island (Shaker Island), called Sha'b 'Abu Nuhâs. The 'base' of this triangular reef runs west to east, with the apex pointing north. This small reef actually has seven confirmed shipwrecks on her and a reputed further three wrecks as yet undiscovered. Sha'b 'Abu Nuhâs is now legendary in diving circles for having the best grouping of wrecks on one reef.

Ranging from west to east along the northwest face of the triangular reef, the most accessible wrecks are: the *Giannis D* located at the west corner; the *Carnatic* located midway along the reef and the *Chrisoula K* near to the east corner of the reef. There are more wrecks on the eastern corner – in fact the *Chrisoula K* was wrecked virtually on top of another two wrecks – but little is known of their origins.

Battered by northern storms, the top of the reef crest is deeply sculpted and indented with fissures. The central lagoon is around 6m (20ft) deep with a sandy bottom and small isolated coral heads popular with feeding stingrays, crocodilefish and flounders. It was while snorkelling along this reef that divers first found evidence of other shipwrecks more ancient than the *Chrisoula K*, the mast and foreparts of which protrude above the water level like the proverbial wreck symbol on an Admiralty chart. These divers found artifacts including copper nails and crockery, indicating that there was another wreck nearby. Shortly thereafter they discovered the wreck of the *Carnatic*.

CARNATIC WRECK

This historic P&O steamship was en route to India when she ran aground midway along northern Sha'b 'Abu Nuhâs on September 12, 1869. Sadly, due to bad judgement (caused by not wanting to abandon the £40,000 worth of coins on board), when the ship broke her back during the night and water rushed into her massive steam-boilers and they exploded – passengers and crew were still on board and 27 lives were lost. It was several days before the survivors were picked up from nearby Shadwan Island. First dived by salvage divers shortly after her sinking, virtually all of the bullion was accounted for. This small discrepancy in

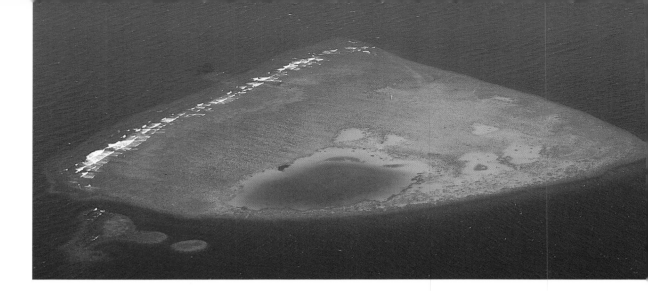

accounting has lured many would-be salvage hunters since (but to no avail). After a period of neglect she was rediscovered by Adrian O'Neil and the crew of the live-aboard boat *Lady Jenny V*, and her identity traced by Lawson Wood.

The *Carnatic* is a wonderful classic shipwreck. Her wooden decking is now long gone, revealing coral encrusted steel ribs. The forward hold still has hundreds of bottles of champagne and soda under the silt.

The wreck now lies on her port side in 21m (70ft) of water, her bows facing east. Her stern and bows are still intact but the central section of the wreck is completely destroyed. The shallower parts of the bows are a swirling mass of glassfish, attended by predatory jacks, lionfish and soldierfish,

while under the shaded areas blue-spotted stingrays can be found.

Completely covered in marine life, but situated in a rather exposed location, the wreck of the *Carnatic* is not dived as often as one would expect it to be, and as a result of this it is still in excellent condition.

ABOVE *An aerial view of Sha'b 'Abu Nuhâs, with surf breaking along the northwestern shore of the reef. The central lagoon is around 6m (20ft) deep with a sandy bottom and small isolated coral heads. Just visible near the eastern end of the northwestern face of the reef is the wreck of the* Chrisoula K. *The* Carnatic *is located further west, near the centre of this face of the reef.*

GIANNIS D WRECK

Just a few hundred metres behind the *Carnatic* on the western reaches of the reef lie the now smashed up remains of the *Giannis D*, which sank in similar circumstances on this reef, after having steered steadily off course during her voyage south from the Suez Canal towards Hodeida in Yemen with a cargo of sawn softwood.

OPPOSITE BOTTOM AND ABOVE *The* Carnatic *is one of the finest wreck dives in the Red Sea. This P&O ship ran aground on Sha'b 'Abu Nuhâs in 1869. Her wooden decking is now long gone, revealing coral encrusted steel ribs (opposite bottom). The lower parts of the bows are a swirling mass of glassfish (above).*

During a terrific storm in April 1983 she hit the reef and her crew abandoned ship. She quickly broke up in subsequent storms, which pounded her relentlessly. Her rear accommodation and engine rooms are still intact, and now also lying on her port side, she is well embedded in the sandy sea bed. Forward from the rear section is a large area of flattened metal sheets, which were once the ship's holds.

Her bows are fairly intact, but only a small section is still recognizable. Over the last 15 years she has been reclaimed by the sea, her masts and rigging covered in corals, her engine rooms filled with glassfish, large groupers patrolling her decks. It is delightful to swim through the open parts of the wreckage surrounded by tropical fish.

CHRISOULA K WRECK

On the eastern approaches of the reef, the former Greek cargo freighter *Chrisoula K* struck Sha'b 'Abu Nuhâs in 1981, carrying a cargo of Italian tiles. Her bow and foremast used to be very obvious markers of this otherwise treacherous reef, but the Egyptian authorities removed the mast (as they deemed it a navigational hazard). In the process they caused excessive damage to the fore section, which was eventually pounded to pieces by subsequent storms as a result of its weakened state.

The rest of the ship is fairly intact; it slopes down the reef crest with the stern at around 30m (100ft). Much of the ship is open, and the wide cargo holds are of particular interest, but penetration of the closed-in parts of the ship is not recommended. The holds can still be explored, but only with the use of underwater lights.

The reef in this area is more sheltered and many parts are of a vertical profile making for a particularly interesting dive. Wreckage from the other ships that have foundered on the same corner of the reef can be found strewn all over this section of Sha'b 'Abu Nuhâs.

NORTHERN RED SEA WRECKS

West of Râs Muhammad is a massive shallow coral reef known as Sha'b el 'Utâf. A tiny string of coral outcrops colloquially called the Alternatives (they were the alternative site to dive when Râs Muhammad was blown out by bad weather) lie between the western end of this reef and Sha'b Mahmûd. Southwest of here is the wreck of the *Dunraven* at Beacon Rock on Sha'b Mahmûd.

To the northwest, the *Thistlegorm* (see page 54) lies east of the southern end of Sha'b Ali and the *SS Kingston* (see page 70) lies just south of Sha'b Ali on Shag Rock. The northern Red Sea is home to some of the most scenic and diveable shipwrecks in the world – as all are well within sport diving depths.

LEFT *A diver explores the wreck of the* Giannis D, *which ran aground during a storm in 1983, near the southwestern corner of the reef. Much of the wreck has been broken up by storms, but the aft section shown here is still relatively intact.*

THE BROTHERS ISLANDS (EL AKHAWEIN)

The Brothers Islands are now open again after being off-limits for three years, though some of the fixed moorings laid by HEPCA have already gone missing. It is now necessary to have Egyptian park rangers on board any boat visiting The Brothers. These two tiny islands rise from deep water 67km (42 miles) off the Egyptian coast just north of El Quseir. The crossing can be rough so choose a heavy boat that is low in the water rather than a more 'modern-looking' one that is high in the water and likely to rock around excessively. Day-boats have dashed out to The Brothers in good conditions, but the weather is unpredictable so this is now discouraged. They are now a live-aboard only destination and are best dived from May to July. The steep walls are not good for safe anchoring so in strong winds and currents your boat captain may be reluctant to stay overnight.

Like Dædalus Reef, The Brothers take the full force of the prevailing winds and currents so they are excellent for pelagic species as well as reef fish, and the strong currents produce wonderful *Dendronephthya* soft tree corals. Big Brother, less than a kilometre (0.6 miles) northwest of Little Brother, is much the larger of the two. Oblong in shape and 400m (1312ft) long, it has a manned British-built lighthouse set just back from the short cliff towards the centre of the southwest face. The drop-off is a wall descending deeper than sport divers should dive, with gorgonian sea whips, sea fans and black corals in the deeper water and colourful soft corals in the shallower water. However, these growths can be found almost everywhere in the Red Sea, and for most divers the main attraction is sharks – grey reef sharks, hammerhead sharks, silvertip sharks, whitetip reef sharks and, in particular, impressive resident oceanic whitetip sharks that like to check out divers. Some divers claim to have seen thresher sharks.

Apart from sharks there are large shoals of fish especially in late spring and early summer when they gather to spawn. These include butterflyfish, snappers, batfish, fusiliers, cornetfish, barracuda, halfbeaks, groupers, jacks, sailfin and black surgeonfish, unicornfish and manta rays.

The wreck of the troop carrier *Aida* II (which sank in 1957) lies bow up, stern down, steeply down the wall at the northwest corner. The bow is at 30m (100ft) and the stern is around 70m (230ft). Nearly 100m (330ft) north of the *Aida* II, an older wreck lies in shallow water. Wreckage, including wheels with spokes, descends from the shallows to 40m (130ft) where the stern has broken off to fall into deeper water. These wrecks are carpeted in stony and soft corals and have lush fish life.

Some divers believe that Little Brother has the better marine life. It certainly appears to be the more colourful, with classic steep walls and deep water on all sides. There are lots of large gorgonian sea fans and *Dendronephthya* soft tree corals and plenty of jacks, tuna, sharks and manta rays, but anemones are surprisingly difficult to find.

LEFT *A sabre squirrelfish* (Sargocentron spiniferum). BELOW *The troop carrier the* Aida II *sank in 1957, near an older, unidentified wreck. Here a diver investigates some of the intriguing debris from the older wreck.* OPPOSITE *Picturesque coral walls near The Brothers.*

ELPHINSTONE REEF (SHA'B ABU HAMRA)

Elphinstone Reef is 12km (7.5 miles) from the Egyptian coast at Marsa Abu Dabbâb. Only about 200m (656ft) long and 30m (100ft) wide and running roughly north-south, the reef does not quite reach the surface. The northern and southern ends of the reef have submerged plateaus; the northern one is shallow, while the southern plateau is much deeper with a drop-off at 30m (100ft) heading down into the depths.

There is no shelter here so the reef can only be dived in good weather. Several diving operations have recently set up in south Egypt and Elphinstone Reef is accessible to their day-boats, so it is best to get here very early in the morning to dive before the other boats arrive. There is really only room for one boat to anchor, and if there is more than one the others must either tie up to the first boat or hold off. Live-aboard boats can find several places inshore that will provide sheltered anchorage for the night.

Elphinstone Reef is normally dived at its southern point for 'The Tomb of the Pharaoh', and a couple of resident oceanic whitetip sharks. A large arch in the coral is found between 50 and 70m (165 and 230ft) and beneath it there is a rectangular section of coral. Most divers suffer from nitrogen narcosis at this depth and a legend has grown around this rectangular section, depicting it as a sarcophagus, the so-called 'Tomb of the Pharaoh'.

With deep near-vertical walls on all sides, the southern point has a narrow shelf at 25m (80ft), which we recently dived looking for hammerhead sharks. As we descended we saw a shoal of more than 20 below the shelf. Three of our dive party chased after them, descending over the drop-off, while the other three of us – conscious that we never achieved good results when photographing hammerheads in deep water – decided to stop above the shelf. This time our luck was in; spooked by the other divers, two large scalloped hammerhead sharks broke away from the shoal, headed up and swam straight over us. With the slow recycling of the

flash gun I only managed to get two photographs before they had gone, but I knew that I had done everything correctly and good hammerhead pictures were on the film.

In addition to hammerhead and oceanic whitetip sharks, the southern end also has silvertip sharks and occasionally silky sharks, while grey reef and whitetip reef sharks are encountered all around the reef.

The much longer east and west sides of the reef have near-vertical walls descending into the depths with an abundance of stony corals, *Dendronephthya* soft tree corals, gorgonian sea fans and sea whips, sponges and black corals. The east wall appears to have the best soft corals. Here, several enormous Napoleon wrasse, circular batfish, Red Sea bannerfish, pennantfish and yellowbar angelfish follow you around. Turtles occasionally swim by, parrotfish dash about and bigeyes, squirrelfish, soldierfish and groupers hover under overhangs and *Acropora* table corals.

DÆDALUS REEF (ABU EL KIZAN)

Now finally re-opened after a few years of being off-limits, Dædalus Reef is a small, isolated reef southeast of The Brothers and 96km (60 miles) off the Egyptian coast between Marsa 'Alam and Gezîret Wâdi Gimâl. Further offshore than most other reefs in the Red Sea, it is a live-aboard only destination and then only dived in summer. The weather can be rough and the crossing quite

FAR LEFT A diver experiences the rich fish life off the deep near-vertical walls of Elphinstone Reef. This relatively small reef – about 200m (656ft) long and 30m (100ft) wide – is also an excellent place to see sharks. LEFT A titan triggerfish (Balistoides viridescens).

uncomfortable if you hit a storm. Preferably use a heavy boat that is low in the water. Dædalus Reef, a danger in the shipping lane, is marked by a British-built lighthouse manned by lonely keepers. It used to be customary to land and cheer them up, but new HEPCA regulations prohibit this. Park rules are enforced by the Egyptian park rangers whom boats visiting Dædalus are obliged to have on board.

The south side offers some shelter for mooring, and experienced skippers can hang-off the lighthouse jetty in the prevailing wind. Rising out of deep water, three sides of the reef are near-vertical walls descending to 70m (230ft) before shelving off further. To the north the prevailing winds and currents bring a profusion of pelagic fish as well as reef fish. Barracuda hover or circle while rainbow runners, snappers, trevallies and tuna dash about and bluespine unicornfish, fusiliers and sailfin surgeonfish school.

To the northeast, northwest and along the east side, you may well see a thresher shark out in the open water, as you drift along lush walls. On the west side, the drop-off is a veritable 'Anemone City' with many attendant clownfish. Angelfish, butterflyfish and circular batfish cruise around while orangespine and spotted unicornfish race about. All sides are richly endowed with stony corals, colourful soft corals, gorgonians and a dense fish life. The current is usually north to south and quite strong to swim against, so it is wise to have a chase-boat pick you up.

The fish life is much the same as that at The Brothers except that there is more of it. The occasional hammerhead shark, grey reef shark or silvertip shark is encountered, together with several whitetip reef sharks and large bottlenose dolphins, but no oceanic whitetip sharks occur here. Inquisitive scrawled filefish and cornetfish follow you closely, while black surgeonfish, jacks

and trevallies are attracted to your exhaust bubbles, which they possibly mistake for small prey. Halfbeaks occur at the surface, blackside hawkfish and various groupers perch on stony coral, and longnose hawkfish lie in ambush among gorgonians.

Unique to Dædalus Reef is a cave at 18m (60ft) on the southwest corner containing some 20 large lionfish. These lionfish approach divers fearlessly and en masse. (I have seen this happen elsewhere, but nowhere else in the Red Sea.) It is not known whether this is a territorial display or a collective technique used by these fish to herd prey when feeding.

In the past there has been shark feeding here, but this is now banned by the new rules.

TOP CENTRE *Elphinstone Reef, which lies about 12km (7.5 miles) off the Egyptian coast at Marsa Abu Dabbâb.*
ABOVE *A coral grouper* (Cephalopholis miniata).
BELOW *A view of Dædalus Reef from the top of the lighthouse showing the long jetty. The new HEPCA rules prohibit landing, but it is only polite to talk to the lonely lighthouse keepers.*

THE SUDAN

CLIMATE

Warm and dry in winter, but offshore winds can be very strong and it is wise to have warm clothes on the boat. In summer it can be unpleasantly hot on land with temperatures of 47°C (117°F). At sea the temperature is comfortable but it is humid.

BEST TIME TO GO

The Sudan is dived all year, but most live-aboard boats operating out of Port Sudan only do so in the winter (when it can get very windy and rough). The best time to go is May–July, and September. Avoid August when rain in nearby Ethiopia causes south winds and *haboobs* (sandstorms).

GETTING THERE

Take a live-aboard boat from Egypt. The air connections are notoriously unreliable, particularly onward from Khartoum to Port Sudan. Direct flights sometime operate from Cairo or Rome, but only in winter.

WATER TEMPERATURE

Averages 28°C (82°F) in summer, 27°C (80.6°F) in winter. There can be highs of 30°C (86°F) in places.

QUALITY OF MARINE LIFE

The greatest density and diversity of species in the Red Sea, with excellent reef fish, gorgonians, stony and soft corals. The absence of large-scale commercial fishing means that there are plenty of pelagic species, especially sharks.

THE SUDAN

SHA'B RUMI

COUSTEAU'S CONSHELF (PRECONTINENT) II

In the early 1960s, Cousteau demonstrated the feasibility of manned underwater habitats. He started with Conshelf I off the island of Pomègues near Marseilles in 1962, and by mid-1963 he had accomplished Conshelf II, which included a star-shaped long-stay habitat at 9m (30ft), a deep habitat at 27m (89ft) and a submarine. This vessel operated from a hangar with a drop-open floor, which enabled it to enter the hangar from below and the water to be pumped out by air pressure so that it could be maintained *in situ*.

Forty kilometres (25 miles) northeast of Port Sudan, Sha'b Rumi (Roman Reef) was selected for the experiments because the sheltered west side combined the necessary reef profile with safe anchorage for the utility vessel *Rosaldo* in the lagoon. A supply gantry was built across the reef and the *Calypso* acted as supply ship. The story of Conshelf II is told in both the book and film *World Without Sun*. When the experiment ended, the habitats were recovered, but everything else remains, evoking the adventures of early underwater pioneers.

Underwater, the scene is reminiscent of a science fiction film set. A large, futuristic onion-shaped steel structure standing on three legs is covered with soft and stony corals. One *Acropora* coral used to be 2m (6.5ft) across, but careless anchoring or diving has removed it. This is the hangar used to garage Captain Jacques Cousteau's saucer-shaped submarine, *DS2*, during his Conshelf II underwater living experiment. The

wooden floor of the hangar has rotted away. The stainless steel plaque beneath it is in memory of a German diver who died at Sha'b Rumi in 1973. The saucer hangar is beside the coral, outside the lagoon, 50m (165ft) south of the more southern of the two lagoon entrances at the northern end of the west side of the reef. The lagoon entrance nearby is only 10m (33ft) wide, so it is difficult for larger live-aboard boats to negotiate during winter's strong north winds. There is safe anchorage inside the lagoon.

Descending to 9m (30ft) we finned between the legs of the hangar, blue-spotted lagoon rays and lionfish darting away as we squeezed up through the entrance hatch. Inside a shoal of sweepers parted for us in panic, our exhaled bubbles distorting our reflections at the interface of the water and a trapped pocket of divers' exhaled air. We stopped for a chat in the 0.5m (20in) air pocket before descending again.

To the north, a low tool shed with a corrugated roof is also covered in coral. East of the shed, a large Napoleon wrasse lurks among massive wire

hawsers and iron grids strewn over the sea floor, while further north, three fish pens with various coloured Plexiglas panels are covered in soft corals and shelter small fish. The pens move during heavy storms. To the west, down the drop-off there is a shark cage and more cables and grids. Today, sharks are only seen deep over the drop-off.

SOUTH POINT

The south point of Sha'b Rumi is famous for its shark population. A superb dive between 20 and 36m (65 and 118ft), where you can see huge shoals of fish and up to 60 sharks at a time, it is similar to the Southwest Point of Sanganeb but has even more prolific fish life. On a recent dive

we experienced several sharks swim directly towards us, while 50 others circled. The leading

ABOVE *The hangar where Captain Cousteau berthed his saucer-shaped submarine, DS2.*
BELOW *Remains of a toolshed at the Conshelf II site.*

shark – one of several large scalloped hammer-heads – had its senses on the air cylinder that I was tapping with my knife, but its eyes on us. The strong current slowed down the animal's graceful approach, allowing us time to focus. We triggered our cameras as it passed overhead, the shark veering off as the flashes fired, but more sharks were following. We cursed the slow recycling of the flash guns – in 30 seconds it was all over and we had only managed a few more shots.

The sharks soon quietened down and resumed circling, the smaller fish reappearing from their hiding places in the coral. We regained our composure, checked the camera equipment and prepared for another close pass.

One of the top dives in the world, the reef wall here drops to 20m (65ft), forming a brilliant mixture of stony and soft corals, and gorgonians interspersed with anthias. The current becomes too much if you try to swim around the corner to the east, however. Below this wall there is a sandy plateau that shelves gently from 20 to 26m (65 to 85ft) while extending south for nearly 100m (330ft) over very deep water.

The smaller prey here attracts predators such as sharks, tuna, rainbow runners, trevally, jacks and large shoals of barracuda. Groups of anything from five to 40 scalloped hammerhead sharks

cruise along the edge, while whitetip reef, grey reef, silvertip and silky sharks and bottlenose dolphins venture over it. Some divers have been intimidated by sharks when snorkelling on the surface, and it is best to ascend close to the reef wall.

Large schools of unicornfish and sailfin surgeonfish hang in the current here, and fusiliers and parrotfish dash about.

The plateau itself is usually sheltered by the upper reef for 30m (100ft) to the south, and angelfish, butterflyfish, enormous Napoleon wrasse and goatfish follow divers around, while squirrelfish and coral and other groupers hang under coral heads. A shark cage, placed at 26m (85ft) by a German film crew in the 1970s, is hardly large enough to enclose a diver. Today the cage is encrusted with coral.

In summer there is a very strong north–south current here, and strong whirlpools are visible on the surface when the current is too strong. You cannot anchor live-aboard boats just across the reef and row to the site as is sometimes suggested. If you want to anchor you will have to do so further north in the lagoon and take a tender out of the lagoon, past the Cousteau site and south to the South Point. It is a long way so you will require a motorized tender.

ABOVE LEFT *Sha'b Rumi South Point is known for its prolific shark population, including hammerheads.*
BELOW *Coral-encrusted, fish-rich reefs at Sha'b Rumi.*
OPPOSITE *Fish pens left by Cousteau shelter small fish.*

SANGANEB

The large atoll of Sanganeb is more than 8km (5 miles) long, rising from very deep water some 27km (17 miles) northeast of Port Sudan. At its southern end there is a lighthouse marking the main shipping channel into Port Sudan. Sanganeb is famous for a profusion of top dive sites, including two of the best in the world; Sanganeb North Point and Southwest Point.

NORTH POINT

The North Point is exposed to the prevailing north winds and currents so it should only be dived in good weather. It is best dived in the early morning when it is calm, as by the afternoon the current will have got up, can be strong and the surface is likely to be choppy.

The point drops off in steps with an exceptionally clean and healthy reef table at 5m (16ft), a sandy platform pointing north with a raised lip at 20m (65ft), and a much larger sandy plateau protruding out further north and shelving from 50 to 60m (165 to 200ft).

The upper reef table is carpeted with stony corals, soft corals and gorgonians, while the reef fish life is as dense and varied as you can find anywhere. Colourful anthias and chromis feed

above the coral, parrotfish and surgeonfish graze the algae and hawksbill turtles eat the sponges. Angelfish and butterflyfish flit around, moray eels peer out of their holes while fusiliers dash about and shoals of bumphead parrotfish charge the coral to break some of it off to eat. In calm conditions divers, snorkellers and especially underwater photographers enjoy this area as there is plenty of light, lots of colour and examples of most of the Red Sea's fish species.

The platform with the raised lip, at 20m (65ft), has lizardfish, gobies with bulldozer shrimps, and damselfish, and often has turtles or a manta ray turning somersaults in a courtship display.

The deeper plateau, shelving from 50 to 60m (165 to 200ft), has large shoals of fish, many of which are pelagic such as tuna, rainbow runners, trevally, jacks, a huge school of barracuda circling in a tight-knit ball, and shoals of juvenile scalloped hammerhead sharks. In the early morning grey reef sharks are found resting on the sand. The visibility is good enough for you to observe these creatures from the outer reef-wall without going deep.

On the east side of the upper reef table there is a large coral head, and below this a wall descends into the depths, resplendent with stony and soft corals, gorgonians, invertebrates and fish life. There is a large old wooden wreck that is covered in whip corals and other gorgonians, but its highest point is at 70m (230ft).

Some 20m (65ft) north of the landmark coral head, you can descend to a small sloping shelf between 40 and 50m (130 and 165ft) deep, which overlooks a much deeper gully to the east. Grey reef sharks, whitetip reef sharks and shoals of more than 40 scalloped hammerhead sharks have been seen cruising this gully. I once had ten juvenile hammerheads swimming around my legs. Huge shoals of blackspotted grunts congregate in small caves here to spawn in April.

SOUTHWEST POINT

Another of the best dives in the world, the southwest point of Sanganeb is sheltered from all but August's southerly winds. In January and February the northerly winds can be so strong that this point and the south wall are the only place outside of the lagoon that one can sensibly dive. At this time I have seen as many as nine manta rays sheltering here.

The upper reef wall has prolific marine life including shoals of sailfin surgeonfish, unicornfish, anthias and chromis. Nooks, crannies and caverns have orange and green *Tubastrea* corals, groupers, bigeyes and soldierfish, while huge

shoals of blackspotted grunts congregate around the caverns in April, to spawn.

As we entered the water on a recent dive, many huge groupers scurried to their hiding places, bluespotted lagoon rays buried themselves in the sand, a coachwhip ray headed off over the eastern edge and a giant (Napoleon) wrasse came up to inspect us. Descending past a large shoal of barracuda we settled just over the drop-off and were rewarded with a close encounter with eight large scalloped hammerhead sharks and several grey and whitetip reef sharks.

Below the reef wall a sandy plateau that is wider than those at Sanganeb's North Point or the South Point of Sha'b Rumi, slopes gently from 20m (65ft) to 36m (118ft), while protruding southwest for 100m (330ft). On the south and west of this plateau the drop-off descends at around 60 to 70° into very deep water, but to the north the drop-off is at a lesser angle. Grey reef and hammerhead sharks patrol the southern edge of this plateau. Lone silvertip or tiger sharks are sometimes encountered and leopard (variegated) sharks have been seen where it joins the South Wall.

Above the plateau there are heads of stony corals, soft corals, gorgonian sea fans and sea whips and every conceivable combination of Red

Sea pelagic and reef fish, most of which are very tame. Large schools of barracuda and rainbow runners shoal while trevally, tuna and jacks prey on smaller fish. Whitetip reef sharks, scorpionfish, stonefish, torpedo (electric) rays and porcupine pufferfish are common. Clownfish nestle in huge anemones, triggerfish guard their nests in the sand and some groupers are so large that they can no longer get out of their caves. The beautifully coloured soft corals fill out when the current is strong.

The site is easily reached by snorkelling from the south jetty of the lighthouse so it is perfect for night diving. Sharks occasionally put in an appearance, but leave you alone. You have to be more careful of tiny juvenile scorpionfish. Spiny lobsters, Spanish dancer nudibranchs, sea hares, hermit crabs with anemones on their shells, banded coral shrimps, snake eels, octopuses, basket stars and tun shells are just a few of the animals on show.

OPPOSITE TOP *Close-up of stylasterid hydrozoan coral* (Distichopora violacea).
OPPOSITE BOTTOM *Grey reef sharks* (Carcharhinus amblyrhynchos) *and a remora* (Echeneis naucrates).
ABOVE *A bluespotted lagoon ray* (Taeniura lymma).
BELOW *Corals on the reef at Southwest Point.*

UMBRIA WRECK

If ever a wreck was designed for the sport diver's pleasure, it is the *Umbria*. Scuttled within the shelter of Wingate Reef off Port Sudan, she can be dived in any weather. There is no current, superb visibility, abundant coral growth and prolific fish life.

Built in 1912 by Reihersts in Hamburg, the twin-engine, twin-propeller, 10,076-ton vessel was originally named *Bahia Blanca*, but was later sold to Lloyd Triestino Di Navigazione Societa Per Azioni and renamed *Umbria*. En route to Rangoon via Eritrea, carrying munitions, aircraft spares, cement and foodstuffs for Italian troops in Eritrea, on 12 June 1940 she was anchored in the sheltered water anchorage outside Port Sudan harbour when Italy formally entered World War II. The British Authorities immediately moved to seize the vessel, but the captain had been warned by radio and ordered the ship's seacocks to be opened.

The British Royal Navy made a survey for possible salvage but judged the munitions unstable when exposed to sea water. In addition the concave reef behind the *Umbria* would deflect a tidal wave into the main harbour if they exploded so the vessel was left intact, marked as dangerous on the charts, and the area was forbidden to shipping.

In 1949 Hans Hass became the first civilian to dive on the wreck and it was his book *Under the Red Sea* and subsequent films that attracted divers, and especially the world's top underwater photographers and cinematographers.

Today the *Umbria* lies at an angle on her port side, with her starboard davits breaking the surface. The port propeller is buried in the coral, but the starboard propeller is clear at 15m (50ft). The stern lies on coral at 20m (65ft), while the bottom of the bow is at 36m (118ft). Penetration of most of the ship is easy; the gangways are clear and the holds are open with munitions, vehicle parts, sacks of cement, bottles of wine, batteries and glass jars scattered around. Entering the engine room and kitchen is more difficult – do not disturb the silt, or you will not be able to see your way out again. Crockery with the Lloyd Triestino emblem and silver serving bowls can still be found in the kitchen.

Spear-fishing, coral and shell collecting have long been banned in Sudanese waters, helping to maintain the wreck's prolific fish life. Bumphead parrotfish, groupers, triggerfish, surgeonfish,

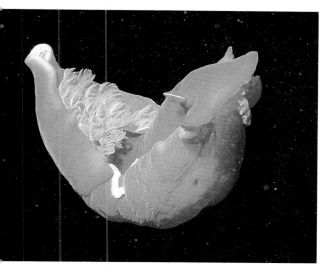

angelfish, butterflyfish, batfish, bream, chub, hawk-fish, lionfish and sergeant-majors are common. Dolphins and turtles pass by in summer and manta rays shelter behind nearby reefs in December and January. I have encountered small whitetip and blacktip reef sharks in the hollow beneath the stern.

Divers have plenty of bottom time to explore the wreck as it is not deep, and snorkellers can enjoy the shallow sections. It is a great night dive. The *Umbria* is one of the most photogenic wrecks in the world, and several Italian film crews have used it as a well-lit set for feature films.

OPPOSITE *The* Umbria *wreck is visible from the surface.*
TOP *A Spanish dancer nudibranch at night.*
ABOVE *A longnose parrotfish* (Hipposcarus harid).
TOP RIGHT AND RIGHT *Munitions (top) and scattered wine bottles (right) in the hold of the* Umbria *wreck.*

careful not to drop the lifeline — if you become disorientated as the sediment is stirred up, it may be your only way to find the way out again.

• Remember that your exhaust bubbles can disturb sediment as well as your fins and hands.

• Be vigilant for parts of the wreck breaking up and be especially careful on wooden wrecks, which often collapse.

• Be vigilant of any sharp metal, which could cut through your lifeline, buoyancy jacket or other equipment if it snags.

• Leave yourself plenty of air to get out of the wreck and back up the shotline.

• If there is a current, deploy a floating rope, drifting freely in the current, from the boat's ascent ladder.

• Even if you have calculated slack water correctly, there may be a strong current running by the time you finish the dive. If this is so, a floating rope from the top of the shotline to the boat's ascent ladder is useful.

• Penetrating large wrecks is advanced diving, and you should be properly trained and equipped. It is unwise to penetrate wrecks at night.

ABOVE   The wreck of the SS Kingston, which ran aground on Shag Rock in the Strait of Gûbal.
BELOW AND OPPOSITE   The photogenic Umbria wreck. A diver (opposite) ascends past the stern section.

TIPS ON WRECK DIVING

• Carry a sharp knife and a suitable monofilament line-cutter or scissors for cutting fishing line and nets.

• Have a good torch and carry another as back up.

• Make sure that all of your equipment is tucked away against your body so that it will not snag anywhere.

• Wear tough gloves.

• Choose slack water to dive a wreck.

• If the wreck is not buoyed, drag a grapnel anchor onto the wreck and buoy the line. The first pair of divers onto the wreck should tie the line off to the wreck, and the final pair of divers up should release it.

• On deep wrecks and in strong currents, arrange a shotline, so that it is as vertical as possible to the part of the wreck that you wish to cover, in order to make the descent and ascent as short as possible. Stage decompression can be carried out on the shotline and spare cylinders fitted with an octopus regulator could also be suspended on it at 10m (33ft) and again at 5m (16ft) for additional safety.

• It is always best to descend and ascend the shotline. Once you leave the shotline on the wreck, make a mental note and take compass bearings of your movements, as a change of tide, or divers stirring up sediment, can produce near-zero visibility. In really bad visibility, fix a distance line from the bottom of the shotline.

• Be extra vigilant as wrecks are often covered with fishing nets and fishing line, visibility is often poor and it is easy to stir up sediment. Wrecks that are badly broken up can be disorientating.

• If you intend to penetrate a wreck, tie back any doors or hatches, so that they cannot close on you in a current. Tie off a lifeline before penetrating and feed it out as you go. Alternatively, tie yourself to the lifeline and have your buddy pay it out as you go through. Don't forget to tie back any further doors or hatches that you enter. Be

CENTRAL INDIAN OCEAN

CLIMATE

The Lakshadweeps and the Andamans receive heavy rain from May–October.

BEST TIME TO GO

Lakshadweeps: November–April.

Andamans: January–May.

GETTING THERE

Lakshadweeps: There is a daily flight to Bangaram from Goa, Cochin or Trivandrum. Flight time is 60–100 minutes. Visitors for the dive centre in Kadmat and Kavaratti take the overnight ship from Cochin. All visitors must be cleared by local government prior to departure.

Andamans: These islands can be reached by live-aboard from Koh Phuket in Thailand, or by flying to Port Blair from Calcutta or Madras on mainland India.

WATER TEMPERATURE

Lakshadweeps: average 24–29°C (75–84°F)

Andamans: average 28–31°C (82–87.8°F).

VISIBILITY

Lakshadweeps: out of the monsoon season visibility is a good 20m (65ft).

Andamans: expect better than 10m (33ft) out of the thermoclines, but worse in the thermoclines.

QUALITY OF MARINE LIFE

Plenty of colourful reef fish in the shallow coral reefs, scores of dolphins and turtles, and, at greater depths, a good range of pelagics. Fairly extensive hard coral bleaching.

SNORKELLING

Good opportunities in both island groups.

INDIA

Fiona Nichols and Paul Lees

LAKSHADWEEP ARCHIPELAGO · THE ANDAMAN ISLANDS

*I*n the vast subcontinent of India, a country not renowned for its diving, there exist two world-class dive destinations which, because of their remoteness, are in pristine condition. The first, and slightly more accessible, is the Lakshadweep Archipelago off the coast of Kerala, southwest India. Long a staging post for mariners in search of spices and sandalwood, Kerala has been a host to Phoenician, Roman, Chinese, Arab, Portuguese, Dutch and English explorers.

Today, visitors arrive by scheduled and charter flights from Europe and Asia, flying directly to Trivandrum and Cochin. Over the centuries foreign cultures have woven their ways into the lives of the local Malayalams, giving the Keralan culture its unique, cosmopolitan outlook.

But it is to the Lakshadweep Archipelago, some 300km (186 miles) west of Kerala, that keen and well-heeled divers travel. This scattering of 12 atolls comprising 36 small islands is the northern geological extension of the Maldives. Of the 36 isles, only ten are inhabited by the local Muslim Malayalams, and foreign visitors are only permitted to stay on a couple of these.

India's second major dive destination is located more than 1000km (620 miles) to the southeast of mainland India, in the Bay of Bengal. A narrow archipelago of more than 300 islands form 'Little India', or, as they are more commonly referred to, the Andaman Islands. Primary rain forest covers around 90 per cent of the island chain, which spreads over an area of around 8240km² (5,155 sq. miles). Twenty-six of the islands are currently inhabited by a total of about 160,000 residents, around a third of whom live in the only town on any of the islands, Port Blair on the east coast of South Andaman Island. Port Blair was originally established to provide sanctuary for the marooned crews of beached vessels.

The main island group comprises five islands, from north to south; North, Middle and South Andaman Island, with the two smaller islands of Baratang and Rutland completing the chain in the south (the latter two being jointly labelled Great Andaman).

Large areas of the islands have been set up as protected parks and reserves, a number of which remain as the homes of numerous aboriginal tribes, and these are strictly out of bounds to outsiders.

To the east of the main island chain lies the uninhabited volcanic mound of Barren Island, one of only two active volcanos in the Indian territories. Beyond this, heading towards the north, lies the coastguard station of Narcondam Island, which oversees the northern approaches. Both of these are popular diving destinations. Sightings of dolphins, dugongs and even swimming elephants are commonplace around the islands.

INDIA

Bangaram Island · *Kadmot Island*

Kavaratti Island ○ · *Kalpeni Island*

Nine Degree Channel

Minicoy Island

LAKSHADWEEPS

Cochin ●

Previous pages A beach on Bangaram Island, in the Lakshadweeps.
Top left A local fishing boat plies the waters around the Lakshadweep Islands.
Opposite An aerial view of Bangaram Island.

LAKSHADWEEP ARCHIPELAGO

The former travel prohibitions and the great distance from the Indian mainland are largely responsible for the excellent natural state of the Lakshadweep Archipelago's reefs, and their abundant indigenous flora and fauna. More than 1000 species of bony fish, plenty of rays and sharks, and dozens of corals and echinoderms are all indigenous to the archipelago.

BANGARAM ISLAND

Such is the calibre of diving in the Lakshadweep Archipelago that one is reluctant to talk about it for, experience shows, the more people who enjoy such perfect diving, the less amazing it becomes! Diving here is in virgin territory and that is its appeal. You really have the idea that you are the first to discover the reefs, and the fact that you are rarely more than one of a dozen divers in the whole area is a wonderful privilege.

Bangaram is a small crescent-shaped island, covered with a coconut palm plantation and clinging to one side of the atoll. There are a couple of other islands, the other side of the atoll, which are within easy reach by hired boat or catamaran.

There is a resort here that can accommodate a maximum of 60 guests. There is little else to do on Bangaram except indulge in watersports, laze in the turquoise waters, hang out in a hammock or wander the dazzlingly white sandy shores. Snorkellers have a wonderful time on the wreck of an old fishing boat, which lies in 3m (10ft) of water in the southeastern part of the atoll. This is now home to various moray eels, a plethora of small reef fish, parrotfish, sea cucumbers and some beautiful corals.

Of the dozen or so dive sites that Bangaram resort divemaster Andreas Heidman has explored, three have proven to be favourites: Shallow Point, Manta Point and Shipwreck.

SHALLOW POINT

Shallow Point is, as its name suggests, a shallow dive not more than 40 minutes by boat from the resort on Bangaram Island. In clear water, 20 to 30m (65 to 100ft) visibility with a light current, there is a wealth of corals. Die-hard snorkellers can also join this trip because, even at the shallower depths, there are plenty of interesting corals to explore, and in among them there are gobies, damselfish, sweetlips, snappers and parrotfish. From time to time, there are stingrays and grazing turtles (turtles are found everywhere in the Lakshadweep Islands). A resident group of garden eels can also be found here, along with a single leopard moray eel. It is a fine dive for

---

ABOVE *A school of inquisitive Oriental sweetlips* (Plectorhinchus orientalis). *The Lakshadweep Archipelago's reefs are little dived and consequently the fish are plentiful and not shy.*

photographers as the visibility is good, and the variety of plants and animals is excellent. This is also a good place for the avid shell-spotter.

MANTA POINT

Favourite among divers early in the season is Manta Point for its manta rays. Although the mantas don't visit all year round, there are plenty of other things to see. This site, just 45 minutes from shore, has an upwelling of water though little current, which brings up fauna from greater depths to feed among the hard corals. The visibility is usually 20m (65ft) or more, and average depth here is around 18m (60ft) though you can go down to 30m (97ft) if the visibility is exceptional. On a good dive there are plenty of schooling fish, barracuda, eagle rays, stingrays

and manta rays will make an appearance. There are usually turtles in the shallows – both green and hawksbill turtles – while the odd whitetip reef shark or nurse shark may swim by. This is not a dive for the macro-photographer.

SHIPWRECK

Some 60 minutes away by boat lie the remains of the *Princess Royal*, an English trading ship dating from 1792. The dive site is simply known as Shipwreck. The wreck lies in approximately 25m (81ft) of clear water and there is usually no current, making it an easy dive. It provides a different marinescape and an unusual alternative to the reef dives that are the norm here. Divemaster Andreas has discovered and salvaged several artifacts, which he gave to the Lakshadweep Museum in the

capital, but you can still see the anchor, four long cannons, pottery shards and some planks that were part of the hull. In and around the wreck there are plenty of fish, though more often solitary or in pairs than in schools, while turtles will occasionally rest in its skeleton. You often encounter a whitetip reef shark nosing around the wreck, and there will usually be stingrays and moray eels. Over the years some hard corals have established themselves around the remains, and these in turn encourage more marine life.

TOP (left to right) *A giant moray eel* (Gymnothorax javanicus); *coral grouper* (Cephalopholis miniata); *blue-lined coral grouper* (Plectropomus oligacanthus). BELOW *A reefscape dominated by plate corals.*

ANDAMAN ISLANDS

The Andaman Islands are surrounded by tropical waters with a plentiful supply of sunlight, which, when coupled with a lack of pollution or fresh water from any mainland, results in flourishing corals. A range of both hard and soft corals occur at all depths. Another factor in the promotion of this healthy environment is that visiting divers are so few and far between that their impact is kept to a bare minimum; there are no permanent dive operators on any of the islands, but makeshift ones do occasionally crop up for short periods of time. The islands are currently only efficiently served by live-aboard excursions visiting from Phuket Island in south Thailand, some 450km (280 miles) to the southeast. As a result of these long distances, trips to the islands are restricted to the season from January to May.

To date, world-class diving sites have been discovered to the north and south of the main island group, especially along the islands' eastern coastlines and offshore islands. That is not to say that there are no prime sites around the other coastlines; these are targets for future exploratory trips.

The diversity of marine life and corals found so far is impressive, with the majority flourishing in shallow waters. There are exciting high-voltage dives along sheer walls and around submerged pinnacles; equally enjoyable is the seemingly

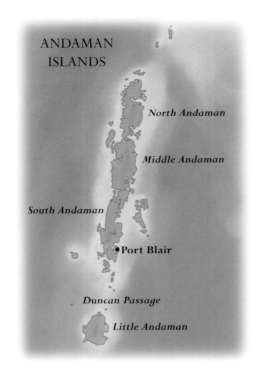

ANDAMAN ISLANDS

North Andaman

Middle Andaman

South Andaman

•Port Blair

Duncan Passage

Little Andaman

endless supply of fringing and offshore reefs. Colourful reef fish abound as do many invertebrates and a selection of turtles. Large pelagics are plentiful too, including a grand variety of sharks. Grey reef, blacktip and whitetip reef sharks are all high on the blue-water sightings list, not to mention the occasional open ocean shark thrown in for good measure. As well as the familiar sight of small reef cleaning stations, there are others that tend to the

demands of much larger visitors such as great barracuda, and a variety of large rays including manta and eagle rays.

NARCONDAM ISLAND

Narcondam Island is located some 135km (84 miles) to the east of North Andaman Island. Its coastline is comprised primarily of rocks, although there is a solitary pebble beach on the island's northwestern tip, behind which sits the coastguard station. Following the headland east takes you past a series of shallow-scooped rocky coves, barely large enough to provide sheltered moorings for anything but the smallest of boats. One, however, remains obviously capable of containing larger vessels and is the dropping off point for one of the best dive sites yet found in the area, Neil's Pride.

NEIL'S PRIDE

This site is actually divided up into three sections. Firstly, and immediately below the water, a gently sloping shelf of plate corals descends to around 20m (66ft). Here the reef is abruptly interrupted by a narrow rocky plateau then a vertical drop-off of around 8m (27ft), and this comprises the second section. Thirdly, and beyond the actual reef, there lies a series of submerged pinnacles that look like gothic statuettes precariously embedded in the gently sloping sea bed. The midpoint of the nearer ones share a similar depth to that of the plateau.

Marine life is plentiful around all three of these sections; the magnificence of the shallower corals is emphasized by a halo of small reef fish, particularly lyretail anthias. The rocky plateau is lavishly punctuated by soft corals and equally colourful reef fish; coral and bluespotted groupers, lunar wrasse and bi-colour parrotfish complement the colours of the corals nicely. Even slumbering turtles are tended to by iridescent cleanerfish.

The deeper and final section of Neil's Pride drops well beyond the limits of sport diving, and a couple of things to be wary of are swirling and downward currents. Curiosity too, can lead divers to exceed planned and safe depths, as this alluring

LEFT *Yellowtop fusiliers* (Caesio xanthonota) *against a typically fish-rich, coral-encrusted Andaman reefscape.*

series of pinnacles continues well into the abyss, with the occasional instance of only a hazy shadowed outline. These are rather splendid and it is easy to wander out and down without realizing actually how much distance you have covered.

The pinnacles serve as cleaning stations, feeding grounds, mating rendezvous and shelter for an immense spectrum of marine life both resident and passing by. Small nooks and crannies provide secluded workshops for a wealth of busy crabs and shrimps as they set about removing parasites from their visitors. The lower sections purvey a majestic appearance as they are fringed with huge gorgonian sea fans, providing shelter and seclusion to flitting Young's gobies and longnose hawkfish. Lastly, manta and devil rays commonly pass by, as do a variety of reef sharks and solitary giant Napoleon wrasse.

BARREN ISLAND

Barren Island certainly is aptly named, with its sloping sides of blackened rocks, rolling ash and hardened larva flowing below the water's edge. These are punctuated by broken and charred tree trunks. The volcanic island is located around 82km (50 miles) east of the southern tip of Middle Andaman and last erupted as recently as 1995 – blasting a crater in its northwest side and rendering it out of bounds to any visitors for three years. Today, wisps of sulphur still hang in the air, courtesy of the occasional jet of yellow steam being forced through the island's barren surface.

As one would expect, the diving here is in complete contrast to other sites found in the area, in that it follows along sheer walls occasionally broken by steep undulating hills of black volcanic soil. Directly off the northwestern point of the island, the seascape drops in places to 80m (275ft), levels out to form a wide canyon, then climbs to reach a narrow crest at a depth of around 40m (137ft). The outer wall of this narrow crest then drops to beyond 120m (410ft). This dive site is known as Computer Drop.

COMPUTER DROP

This location is an enjoyable feature dive, even though there are not many corals. However, there are small tables of staghorns and in the deeper waters, black sea fans and bushes of white stinging hydroids. The almost slate-like walls and the deep ledges are lent colour by radiant feather and basket stars, and splashes of orange and blue encrusting sponges. The majority of reef fish along the walls, although colourful, tend to be on the small side. Typically, the angelfish and butterflyfish remain in their juvenile stages. A handful of species that break this trend include Napoleon wrasse, schools of orangespine unicornfish and powder-blue surgeonfish. The ashen slopes dissecting the drop-offs are punctuated by numerous unidentified gobies and their symbiotic hosts, blind alpheid shrimps, which make hasty retreats into their burrows if approached.

The depths of this underwater canyon are almost constantly patrolled by large sharks, including blacktip, greytip and whitetip reef sharks, silvertips and, on rare occasions, oceanic species that appear suddenly from the depths to investigate – and startle – any human visitors!

Away from the wall, large schools of other pelagics rise from the abyss in search of prey. There are regular sightings of dogtooth tuna, great and chevron barracuda, and rainbow runners.

CENTRE *A juvenile emperor angelfish* (Pomacanthus imperator). *It has very different markings to an adult, so that adult males do not see it as a threat sexually.*
BELOW *A yellow feather star adds a burst of colour to a reefscape festooned with soft corals and sea fans, and covered in lyretail anthias* (Pseudanthias squamipinnis).

MALDIVES

Sam Harwood and Rob Bryning

NORTH MALE ATOLL · ARI ATOLL · FELIDHU ATOLL

The tiny island nation of the Maldives divides the otherwise uninterrupted currents that flow across the Indian Ocean. This magnificent chain of atolls stretches 868km (539 miles) from north to south and is just 130km (80 miles) wide. To the north lie the Lakshadweeps and to the south the Chagos Islands; all are part of the same ridge that rises 3000m (9840ft) from the Indian Ocean floor.

The 1200 or so islands of the Maldives are grouped geographically into 26 ring-shaped reefs called atolls. Each atoll encloses a shallow lagoon with a flat sandy bottom at relatively shallow depths ranging from 35 to 85m (115 to 280ft). Around the atoll perimeter runs the outer reef, which plunges down steeply to the depths of the ocean. The reef is intermittently broken by channels that allow oceanic water to flow into and out of the central lagoon. It is these channels that provide the unique dive sites that make Maldivian diving so special.

The northern region of the central Indian Ocean is the only ocean in the world with a current pattern that changes twice a year, under the influence of the monsoon winds. To appreciate the diving and the dive sites of the Maldives it is essential to take into account these two distinct seasons. Regardless of the season, however, if you are diving on the windward side of the atoll where the currents are flowing in from the ocean, you will experience excellent visibility and wonderful diving. It is these ocean currents that bring food and vitality to the reefs.

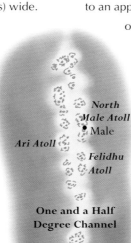

North Male Atoll
Male
Ari Atoll
Felidhu Atoll
One and a Half Degree Channel
Addu Atoll

Divers visiting the Maldives will find that their dives can be grouped into three main types of site. On the outer reef of the atoll divers can enjoy drift dives along the outer wall that slopes steeply down to an apparently bottomless ocean. A great variety of reef life can be seen on such a dive and a glance into the blue may be rewarded with the sight of sharks, huge tuna, sailfish or dolphins.

Perhaps the most adrenaline-charged of the dive sites are the channels that break the perimeter of the atoll. Oceanic waters flow into these narrow channels bringing with them a great concentration of microscopic life that is the staple diet for a vast number of fish that inhabit the reefs. It is as if an invisible line has been drawn across the mouth of the channels; the reef fish swim to the very edge to greet the nutrient-rich waters, and for their own protection they school in huge numbers, for just off the mouth of the channel their pelagic predators are also waiting for an easy meal. While most of these fish are relatively unaffected by it, hard coral bleaching after the 1997/1998 El Niño is extensive.

The third type of site that divers will experience in the Maldives is the *thila*. This is a small, submerged reef usually situated in the middle of a channel (they are also found well inside the atoll). Most *thilas* are oval in shape with their reef top at eight to 10m (26 to 33ft) and their sloping sides dropping down to the atoll floor at 35 to 40m (115 to 130ft). A *thila* creates an oasis for marine life of all sizes and provides some great diving.

Opposite The Maldives is known for its beautiful palm-fringed beaches and unspoilt islands.
Top right Locally built *dhonis* at anchor at a typical island resort.

CLIMATE
Tropical: it is hot and humid throughout the year with land temperatures of 25–30°C (72–80°F). There is an average rainfall of 215mm (8.5in) per month in the wet season (May–October), and 75mm (3in) per month in the dry season (November–April).

BEST TIME TO GO
January–April and August–September.

GETTING THERE
International flights, both chartered and scheduled, to the airport close to Male.

WATER TEMPERATURE
28–29°C (82–84°F) throughout the year.

VISIBILITY
20–30m (65–100ft)

QUALITY OF MARINE LIFE
Prolific and varied.

DEPTH OF DIVES
From surface dives to 40m (130ft).

SNORKELLING
The snorkelling is excellent throughout the Maldives, in both seasons.

PRACTICALITIES
Most of the best dive sites are only accessible by boat, and many of these are visited only by live-aboards. In the wet season winds and currents come predominantly from the west. This can be the season of strong winds and the selection of dive sites may be somewhat restricted to the lee sides of the atolls and reefs.

SEASONAL VARIATIONS IN THE MALDIVES

There are two distinct seasons in the Maldives, and it is vital to understand them in order to get the most out of diving here.

THE DRY SEASON
From the month of November until April the Maldives experiences its driest season, during which diving conditions are considered to be at their optimum, with light winds and currents coming from the northeast. At this time of year, clear ocean water flows into the atolls from the east, bringing with it superb fish life and creating thrilling diving opportunities.

THE WET SEASON
The period from May to October is described as the wet season, with winds and currents coming predominantly from the west. The diving during these months is still fabulous, although this can be the season of strong winds and the selection of dive sites may be restricted to the lee sides of the atolls and reefs.

ABOVE *An aerial view of a typical atoll.*
BELOW (left to right) *A pair of the nocturnal blotch-eye soldierfish* (Myripristis murdjan); *a yellowmask angelfish* (Pomacanthus xanthometopon); *a hump-back unicornfish* (Naso brachycentron).

Whatever the season, however, dive sites on the windward sides of the atolls, where the currents are flowing in from the ocean, will guarantee you excellent visibility and wonderful diving. You will be diving in the Indian Ocean currents that bring vitality to these fish-rich reefs.

Although there are 26 atolls in the Maldives, diving is officially restricted to 11 of them. In reality, however, the diving zone covers a huge area and there are still a great many unexplored reefs as well as hundreds of identified sites.

The sites that have become well known are those that are easily accessed from the main tourist atolls. These are North Male Atoll, Ari Atoll and Felidhu Atoll.

ABOVE AND BELOW *The striking collare, or red-tailed butterflyfish (Chaetodon collare). These collare butterflyfish are often seen in pairs and sometimes (below) in schools, feeding on coral polyps.*

NORTH MALE ATOLL

This is a large atoll, home to the capital of the Maldives (Male) and the international airport. There are 27 resort islands in this atoll, most of which are concentrated in its southern region. Although this is a busy atoll, North Male has some of the best dive sites in the Maldives.

GIRIFUSHI THILA (HP REEF)

Located in the channel between Himmafushi Island and Girifushi Island, this *thila* offers divers one of the best and most diverse dive sites in the Maldives. The main *thila* rises from the atoll bed from 35m (115ft) up to 12m (40ft), and it is made up of enormous house-size boulders that form numerous cracks and crevices, overhangs and caves. Every available surface of the *thila* is covered in iridescent orange, blue and yellow *Dendronephthya* soft coral, and there are great quantities of sea fans and black coral trees.

At one point of the reef there is a tunnel formed between the rocks that looks like a chimney rising from 25m (80ft) to the reef top at 12m (40ft).

As the currents flow in and out of the atoll, providing vital food for the soft corals, it also provides the perfect environment for reef fish to shelter and for pelagic fish to hunt. At the point where the current hits the reef divers can see a spectacular variety of fish life including eagle rays, prowling tuna and barracuda. There are also often schooling grey reef sharks.

Girifushi Thila is best dived in the early morning during the dry season (November until April) when the current is flowing in from the east. Strong currents are often encountered here and divers should jump into the water well up-current of the *thila*.

As with all dive sites in the Maldives, the main underwater action will be at the point where the current hits the reef and divers wishing to see sharks and other pelagics should spend plenty of time in this area. For a variety of colour and smaller fish and invertebrate life, the many caves and overhangs around the sides of Girifushi Thila are quite spectacular.

This is a protected marine site which means that no fishing is allowed to take place here.

BODUHITHI THILA

During the dry season Boduhithi Thila is a fantastic place to observe manta rays and whale sharks feeding in plankton-rich waters. They cruise the thermoclines with their mouths agape, filtering the water like giant vacuum cleaners.

Boduhithi Channel is in the region of 0.5km (0.3 miles) wide, and in places up to 40m (130ft) deep. There are several large *thilas* in the channel and all of them are good for manta spotting. However, the best *thila* is the one nearest to the ocean drop-off, which may not be the most attractive in terms of its reef top, but which is perfectly situated within the current to attract the mantas wishing to feed on the outflowing tide.

At certain stages of the running of the tide, it seems there is a natural upwelling of cooler water on the ocean drop-off. As the warmer atoll water flows out of the channel, a thermocline is created,

trapping plankton-rich waters. When this happens, both manta rays and whale sharks can be seen filling their bellies, and divers and snorkellers return to their boats thrilled.

The manta rays on Boduhithi Thila can be seen cleaning as well as feeding. Their cleaning stations are the massive corals set close to the ocean front near the centre of the *thila*. The mantas line up, waiting their turn at the cleaning station. When it is all clear, they glide in and hover over the coral

massif. The cleanerfish then set to work, dashing into the mouth and gill cavities, nibbling at the small organisms and debris that have become attached to the manta. This cleaning ritual provides an opportunity to spend hours in the presence of the gentle manta ray, but divers hovering above the massive corals of the cleaning stations will prevent the mantas from coming in. Instead, divers should stay low on the reef and position themselves around the perimeter of the large corals.

ABOVE *There are also good wreck dives in the Maldives, such as the* Skipjack *wreck near Kuredu Island.*
RIGHT *Grey reef shark* (Carcarhinus amblyrhynchos).

RASFARI

Rasfari is located on the northwest corner of North Male, and in the wet season clear oceanic currents travel across the Indian Ocean and flow directly

---

ABOVE *Soft corals and* Tubastrea *compete for space.*
RIGHT *A Vlaming's unicornfish* (Naso vlamingii).
BELOW *A cleverly camouflaged whitespotted grouper*
(Epinephelus caeruleopunctatus).

into this part of the atoll. The best part of the dive is a small *thila* that sits on a plateau with its reef top at 25m (80ft). The plateau is perched on the edge of a huge drop-off and sits about 70m (230ft) away from the main perimeter reef.

Although it may be difficult to reach in strong currents, it really is worth the effort as the *thila* is a magnet for big fish, especially eagle rays and some huge barracuda, and also grey reef and silvertip sharks. On a good day you may see a wall

of 25 grey reef and whitetip reef sharks with a squadron of eagle rays among them.

Over the edge of the drop-off at 40m (130ft) is a section of caves with a beautiful arched swim-through. All the caves are full of soft corals, sea fans and black coral trees and sometimes a giant grouper can be seen here, piloted by three or four tiny, striped juvenile jacks. Between the *thila* and the main reef there are some fabulous sand-filled gullies where garden eels in their hundreds sway in the current. Here, whitetip reef sharks often clean and rest and stingrays can be found camouflaged beneath the sand. Opposite the *thila*, on top of the main reef, there is an unusual coral and sand formation that resembles a swimming pool. Nearly 100m (330ft) long and 50m (164ft) wide, this sand-filled pool attracts an interesting array of marine life. Rasfari is not as rewarding in the dry season.

ARI ATOLL

Lying 50km (30 miles) west of Male, Ari Atoll was one of the first atolls to be developed for tourism. There are now 27 resorts within the atoll and many of the most famous Maldivian dive sites are located here.

MADIVARU (HAMMERHEAD POINT)

One of the great joys of diving in the Maldives is the variety of marine species that can be seen in its waters. At one site divers can enjoy the thrill of grey reef sharks, at another site the spectacle of manta rays feeding, and here at Madivaru there is the possibility of a blue-water encounter with the elusive hammerhead shark.

This is a challenging dive, not least because the ideal time of day for the dive to take place is at sunrise. In addition, it is a blue-water dive and often divers cannot see the reef with which to orientate themselves. Madivaru, located in the tiny Rasdhu Atoll in the northern part of Ari, is a narrow channel that faces the ocean, and it is surrounded by exceptionally deep water.

Once in the water, divers swim out towards the sunrise leaving the reef behind them. The hammerheads are most often seen at a depth of 25 to 35m (80 to 115ft). Their habitat is the open ocean, although they may hunt near reefs. The experience of seeing schooling hammerheads is electrifying, and once divers swim into their territory these impressive sharks – first seen as shadows in the blue – become more and more curious to inspect the intruders.

MAAYATHILA

This is a very famous dive site in the Maldives, best known for its resident school of grey reef sharks that frequently thrill visiting divers, and in addition, there is a huge variety of other marine life living on the *thila*. Located just inside the atoll perimeter of the northeastern part of Ari, the site is exposed to nutrient-rich ocean currents that flow into the channel. It is small enough, 30m (100ft) in diameter, that you can swim around it easily in one dive but, as always, it is the point of the current that concentrates the underwater activity.

When you first jump in, where the current hits the reef, it is the density of the fish life that is most impressive. A huge school of swarming fusiliers will be constantly darting and surging to avoid the stealthy attacks of the dogtooth tuna and packs of jacks. Add to this the grey and whitetip reef sharks, turtles, stonefish, frogfish,

ABOVE *The inhabited island of Dangheti in Ari Atoll is often visited by tourists staying on resort islands nearby.*
LEFT *A fire goby* (Nemateleotris magnifica), *with its distinctive elongated first dorsal spine.*
BELOW *Soft corals are abundant in the Maldives.*

honeycomb morays, batfish and the many, many other species that are seen on Maayathila, and you are in for a truly superb dive.

The topography of the reef is also very interesting, with many caves, overhangs and outcrops to be explored. North of the *thila* there is a large satellite rock that is well worth a visit. Its vertical sides drop down to the atoll floor at 40m (130ft), and it is covered in many species of soft corals as well as some huge black coral trees. Divers can often see a large school of goggle-eyes and chevron barracuda here, lurking just off the point, in the current.

The channel between the satellite rock and the *thila* is where the grey reef sharks often patrol. To the south of the *thila* is another, smaller satellite rock, which is also an interesting point of the dive, although on this side of the *thila* the coral growth is quite poor.

Maayathila is one of the most exhilarating night dives in the Maldives. The fusiliers that are seen swarming in the blue water during the day, look to the shelter of the cracks and crevices of the reef for safety at night. There are more fish than places to hide, and the dark brings an opportunity for the sharks and moray eels to seek out their prey. Divers can observe as the sharks swim frantically in and out of their torch beams, snapping at the hapless fusiliers.

KUDARAH THILA

Situated in the Dhigurah Channel in the southeast corner of Ari Atoll, is the beautiful site of Kudarah Thila. The topography of the reef is unusual and fascinating and the *thila* has the great advantage that it is an excellent dive in both the wet and the dry seasons, and in almost all but the very strongest of currents.

Rising from the atoll floor at around 40m (130ft) is a large plateau consisting of four huge coral heads that come up to within 12m (40ft) of the surface. As Kudarah Thila is no more than 100m (330ft) in diameter, divers can swim around the whole site in one dive. Each of the coral mounds is undercut from 15 to 25m (50 to 80ft) with superb caves. It is well worth your while to explore these caves, as they are positively jammed full of colourful soft corals, whip corals and other gorgonians.

The gulleys that have formed between the four coral mounds lead into a central basin that harbours huge quantities of fish life, including an enormous school of blue-lined snapper. Watch out for the yellow trumpetfish that shadow the snapper while hunting on the reef.

Grey reef sharks, large groupers, giant trevally and schools of rainbow runners can be seen where the current hits the reef. This is an absorbing, many-faceted dive.

ABOVE *A close-up of a giant anemone (Entacmaea quadricolor)* showing the bulbous stinging tentacles that provide refuge for a number of clownfish species. BELOW *The green feather star clings to the reef and feeds off plankton that it catches in its feathery arms.*

HUKURUELHI FARU

No dive trip to the southern part of Ari Atoll during the dry season would be complete without a visit to the manta point in the Hukuruelhi Faru (more commonly known as Madivaru). This is a particularly good place to watch manta rays as the gently sloping reef provides the perfect environment for them to take advantage of the hundreds of cleaner wrasse living on the reef top.

In the dry season, when the current flows out of the Hukuruelhi Channel, it carries with it large quantities of plankton. The mantas are drawn to the area by the abundance of food in the water and divers can see them in large numbers feeding on the surface as well as being cleaned. Whale sharks are also attracted to the area during the same period and, although they are not reef-dwelling creatures, the narrow topography of the channel and the current patterns brings them in close to the reef.

LEFT *This complex reefscape is an excellent example of the quality of the dive sites in the Maldives. This is why a hard core of divers return again and again — either relaxing on the many resort islands, or leading an existence almost totally dedicated to diving on one of the many good live-aboards that operate here.*

BELOW *A brittle star uses a gorgonian whip coral to gain access to plankton carried by in the current.*

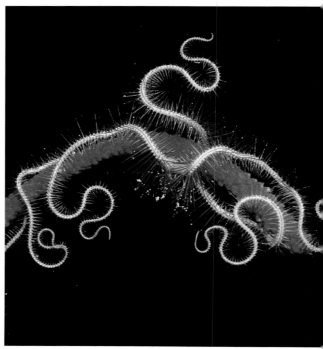

FELIDHU ATOLL

This unusually shaped atoll, located 56km (35 miles) from Male's international airport, offers a style and variety of diving that is different from the *thilas* and reefs of the more developed North Male and Ari atolls. With just two resort islands, Felidhu Atoll remains unspoilt and enjoys a remote peace.

MIARU KANDHU

Miaru means 'shark' in Dhivehi and this is definitely a big-fish dive. It is a challenging dive as a result of the strong currents that flow into the atoll in the dry season.

Miaru Kandhu (*kandhu* means channel in Dhivehi) is approximately 100m (330ft) wide and 30m (100ft) deep. The front of the channel faces the ocean on the east side of Felidhu Atoll, and drops down vertically into the ocean blue. Swimming across the mouth of this channel at 30m (100ft), following the atoll floor, divers often encounter large numbers of grey reef sharks, huge squadrons of eagle rays dancing in the current, and large patrolling tunas. Hammerhead sharks can also be seen out in the ocean, cruising the entrance to the channel.

It is a great experience for a diver to swim out into the centre of a channel like this without being able to view the reef on the other side, and yet be perched above a sheer drop-off in a marine wilderness of big-fish life.

In the dry season, the eastern side of Felidhu Atoll offers truly wonderful channel diving. The boot-like shape of the atoll acts like a funnel for the prevailing northeasterly currents, drawing them into the channel along with the nutrients they carry and a great quantity of interesting and colourful fish life, and at the same time providing crystal clear visibility.

In the wet season, when the current is flowing out of the channels, Miaru Kandhu loses its clear water and shark action, but the inner reef corner is still a good place to watch manta rays coming in to be cleaned.

INSET *Orangestriped triggerfish* (Balistapus undulatus). RIGHT *A school of yellowspot emperorfish* (Gnathodentex aurolineatus) *resting. They feed at night.* BELOW *Cuttlefish* (Sepia officinalis vermiculata) *are not fish at all, but molluscs. Related to squid and octopuses, they have good vision and can change colour. If threatened, they darken, eject a dark ink, then become light again and escape by moving backwards.*

FOTEYO KANDHU

Foteyo Kandhu, or channel, is located on the fringing reef that is the easternmost point of the Maldives. In the dry season, clear oceanic waters flow in through the narrow channel, accentuating the stunning beauty of this site.

The channel is approximately 200m (656ft) wide but is divided into two narrow passages by a large *thila* that shallows to within 3m (10ft) of the surface. The front of the channel is a vertical wall that drops down thousands of metres to the bed of the Indian Ocean.

On the drop-off of the western passage is a stack of caves and overhangs that begins at 20m (65ft) and continues on to more than 50m (164ft). The ceilings of the caves are festooned with beautiful, iridescent orange, blue and yellow soft corals, and the caverns themselves are packed with fish life. Divers venturing onto this immense wall in the early morning may be rewarded by the sight of schooling hammerheads.

In fact, this is an area where you may see any kind of pelagic species, so divers should always keep an eye on the open ocean. The eastern passage has a white sandy bottom at 16m (52ft) and is commonly known as Triggerfish Alley, as large, yellowmargin triggerfish build their nests here and defend their territory ferociously.

During the wet season the visibility in the channel is reduced but it is still a magnificent dive and manta rays are often seen feeding on the out-flowing current and being cleaned above the coral heads on the shallow reef top. Of course, the site is at its very best in the dry season, and when the current is flowing in from the ocean visibility is at its best.

In both seasons, pods of dolphins migrating from ocean to atoll are regularly seen or heard by divers and snorkellers.

LEFT *A typical manta cleaning station consists of a massive coral head set close to the ocean floor and inhabited by numerous cleaner wrasse and anthias. Manta rays will hover over a coral head like this one while the cleaner fish set about their work, picking off parasites and debris.*

FOLLOWING PAGE *Soft corals and a host of small reef fish adorn a stunning Maldives reefscape.*

TURTLES

Turtles are relics from a prehistoric time when reptiles ruled the seas and the land. They have survived into modern times despite the risks involved in laying their eggs on land. The eggs are vulnerable to man and other predators and the hatchlings have to run the gauntlet of crabs and sea birds before they reach the ocean, where sharks and fish snap them up in the shallows. To compensate for this, females lay hundreds of eggs during a breeding season.

In the ocean the weight of their bulky, protective shells is offset by the buoyancy of sea water and they become highly efficient swimming machines. Juvenile turtles drift near the surface in mats of seaweed and feed on floating animals. The adults feed on the bottom and in inshore areas. Loggerhead turtles eat snails, mussels, crayfish, crabs, sea urchins and even fish, whereas adult leatherback turtles feed exclusively on jellyfish. Adult green turtles feed on algae and sea grasses.

Of the seven species of living marine turtles, five occur in the Indian Ocean region, including the smallest, the Olive Ridley turtle. Leatherbacks are the largest of these turtles, growing up to 178cm (70in) long.

ABOVE LEFT *A clutch of young turtles swim through the shallows in the Maldives.*
ABOVE *A hawksbill turtle (Eretmochelys imbricata) feeding on sponges.*

BELOW *A large green turtle (Chelonia mydas) hauls itself back to sea after laying its eggs on a beach in Western Australia. It is unusual for such a turtle to be ashore in daylight as laying is usually done at night.*

CHAGOS ARCHIPELAGO

Charles Anderson

SALOMON ATOLL • PEROS BANHOS ATOLL • GREAT CHAGOS BANK

hagos, an isolated group of atolls and reefs in the central Indian Ocean, lies 480km (300 miles) south of the Maldives and about 1600km (1000 miles) from the nearest land (Sri Lanka). This is one of the world's least accessible places.

The Chagos Archipelago consists of five atolls and 10 reefs and submerged shoals. In all there are about 50 islands, which in general appearance are very similar to those of the Maldives. The southernmost atoll, Diego Garcia, holds a US military base. The other islands are uninhabited. Because of the military presence, the whole archipelago is off-limits to most would-be visitors. Dive charters are not allowed. For the diver there are only three ways to get there: join the military; go on a private yacht; or go as part of an official scientific expedition.

The Chagos islands were long known to Maldivians and by Arab seafarers, but they were largely ignored until the coming of the Europeans. After discovery by the Portuguese in the early 16th century, increasing use was made of them. First they were used as a stopping-off and watering place for sailing ships, then as a site for coconut plantations, briefly as a coaling station for steamships, and later as a strategic military base.

The names of the islands reflect the ebb and flow of European maritime empires. The atoll

Peros Banhos Atoll

Salomon Atoll

Three Brothers

Great Chagos Bank

Diego Garcia Atoll

CHAGOS ARCHIPELAGO

names Diego Garcia and Peros Banhos were bestowed by early Portuguese navigators. Islands frequented by plantation workers bear down-to-earth French names, like Île de la Passe, Île Poule and Île du Sel. Exposed islands and isolated reefs, thoroughly explored for the first time by British naval chart makers in the 1830s, were left proud military names like Victory Bank, Nelson's Island and Blenheim Reef.

Both the French and the British laid rival claim to the islands in the latter part of the 18th century, with the French establishing coconut plantations on several islands. However, the capture of Mauritius (from where the French had administered Chagos) in 1810 left the islands firmly in British control, a position that was ratified in the Treaty of Paris in 1814. Chagos has remained a British possession to this day, and is now officially known as the British Indian Ocean Territory.

In 1966 a 50-year defence agreement was signed between the UK and the USA, granting the USA use of the islands for defence purposes. Under the agreement, no commercial activities are allowed in the islands. To meet this requirement the coconut plantations were closed and the plantation workers were forcibly deported to Mauritius. The old plantation workers' cemetery on Île Boddam in Salomon Atoll, and the plantation factory ruins on Île du Coin in Peros Banhos Atoll, are mute reminders of a lost way of life.

Opposite The striking longfin bannerfish (*Heniochus acuminatus*).
Top right A beach on the Île de la Passe

CLIMATE
Hot and tropical. Southeast trade winds blow strongly from about May–September. From October–April there are light to moderate winds, mainly from the northwest. The warmest time of year is March/April, with average temperatures of 29–30°C (84–86°F). The coolest time is July–September, with average temperatures of 26–27°C (79–80.6°F).

BEST TIME TO GO
Calmest conditions from January–April. July is also reported to be relatively calm.

GETTING THERE
Not easy! The military air base at Diego Garcia is off-limits to most people, but has been used by approved scientific expeditions. The best option is to go by private yacht.

WATER TEMPERATURE
25–31°C (77–88°F).

VISIBILITY
Good, up to 30m (100ft). May be less than 15m (50ft) within atolls at some times.

QUALITY OF MARINE LIFE
Very good. Similar to that of the Maldives, but with interesting differences including an endemic anemonefish and coral species. There has been bleaching of hard corals.

SNORKELLING
Excellent.

DEPTH OF DIVES
All dives are reef dives. Dive depths range from about 2–40m+ (6.5–130ft+). Outer atoll slopes drop to the ocean floor.

Divers who do manage to find their way to the Chagos today will find the diving very similar to that in Maldives. The reef forms are essentially the same, as are most of the corals and fish. However, there are a few fascinating differences. For one, the submerged 'offshore' reefs that are so common in the Chagos are absent from the Maldives. Also, the Chagos is home to a couple of marine animals found nowhere else in the world.

One is the Chagos brain coral, known scientifically as *Ctenella chagius*. Most corals have enormous geographical ranges, so why this species, which is common in Chagos, should be restricted to such a small area is a mystery. Another species found only in these islands is the Chagos anemonefish (clownfish), *Amphiprion chagosensis*. Like all anemonefish it lives exclusively in partnership with a giant sea anemone, in this case the magnificent sea anemone, or *Heteractis magnifica*.

SALOMON ATOLL

Salomon is a relatively small atoll, only 8km (5 miles) long, but it is almost entirely enclosed. As a result it offers particularly safe anchorage and is the favourite of visiting yachtsmen. The single entrance channel on its northern side is wide but shallow, only six to 8m (20 to 26ft) deep. This channel offers some great diving. An in-current brings clear water from outside, and a modicum of safety too as the current will carry you into the atoll and not out into the ocean if you do miss your boat cover!

At the outer edge of the channel, the reef drops steeply away. Near the edge are superb table corals, which are replaced by beautiful sea fans further down the slope. Look out here for the Chagos anemonefish, which seems to prefer reef slopes to shallower reef flats. This is also a likely place for sharks, although even in Chagos shark numbers have been affected by illegal fishing.

A feature of Salomon is that the atoll basin is relatively shallow. It is mostly less than 20m (65ft), well within easy diving range, and quite unlike the much deeper basins of Peros Banhos Atoll and Great Chagos Bank. Perhaps because it is so

shallow, much of the floor of Salomon Atoll is carpeted with rich coral growths. So wherever you are in Salomon, a dive on the anchor is always worth a try (but do not anchor directly over corals!). Keep a look out for turtles. In coral-rich Salomon Atoll (and Peros Banhos), hawksbill turtles are particularly common. This is in contrast to Diego Garcia lagoon, where there are luxuriant and extensive beds of sea grass, and green turtles are plentiful.

PEROS BANHOS ATOLL

Peros Banhos is a larger and more open atoll than Salomon, but safe anchorages can be found tucked in near the islands on the western side. Several islands on the eastern side are important sea bird nesting islands, and there is talk of making them (and the waters in their immediate vicinity) nature reserves.

MAPOU GARDEN

In the northwestern corner of Peros Banhos Atoll, Île Diamant offers a sheltered anchorage. From here you can dive in the large channel entrance or

---

LEFT *A hard coral seascape of staghorn corals.*
ABOVE *A hawksbill turtle* (Eretmochelys imbricata).
OPPOSITE LEFT *A beautiful sea slug* (Nembrotha *sp.*).
OPPOSITE RIGHT *Colourful ascidians off Peros Banhos.*

on the steep outer atoll reef to the north. However, my favourite dive site is a small sheltered reef on the inside on Île Mapou, just to the south. Here a calm shallow embayment offers extended bottom time among rich corals interspersed with white sand patches. This is ideal territory for the macro-photographer hunting obscure wrasses and gobies, and also for searching out pretty nudibranchs and flat worms.

VIENNA ROCK

In the southwestern corner of the atoll, the diving near Île du Coin is excellent, with some large bommies (coral heads) just to the north being well worth a look. However, my favourite site, christened 'Vienna Rock' in honour of a young yachting couple from Austria who told me about it, is on the northern side of Île Vache Marine. It is a coral rock pinnacle reaching up from about 15 to 8m (50 to 26ft), and it is plastered with marine life. Thick growths of gorgonians sprout from the walls, and in their shade a rich carpet of sponges and ascidians provides a rich hunting ground for the macro-photographer.

GREAT CHAGOS BANK

Great Chagos Bank is a vast maze of coral reefs. Most of them are submerged with only a few parts reaching the surface. The bank is not normally classified as an atoll by reef scientists, because so much of it is submerged, and its origins are not well understood. If it is a true atoll, albeit one that is partly drowned, then it is by far the largest atoll

in the world. Its total area is roughly 18,100km² (7,000 sq. miles). To put this into perspective, the total area of all the atolls in the Maldives is roughly 20,700km² (8,000 sq. miles).

There are only eight islands on the bank, all confined to the northern and western perimeter. Most are important nesting and roosting islands for sea birds. As a result they are being considered as potential nature reserves, which would make access to the islands and adjacent reefs illegal without special permission.

THREE BROTHERS

This is a group of small islands on the western side of the bank. In fact, there are four islands in the Three Brothers: the fourth one appears to be of recent origin, as it was not charted in the survey of 1837, nor was it mentioned on earlier French charts on which the group was originally dubbed Les Trois Frères. This newcomer is no more than a bare sea bird roost of sand and coral rubble, appropriately name Resurgent.

Because the atoll rim of Great Chagos Bank is not complete, big ocean swells crash in on the Three Brothers from all sides, even on calm days. Depending on the conditions at the time, there may be no sheltered side to anchor on. One

possible anchorage is on the extreme southeastern side of the reef of Middle Brother. This will put you right next to a rich coral wall and over a flat sand and coral reef step in 18m (60ft). Getting in could not be simpler – jump straight off the boat into a coral-lined swimming pool with 30m (100ft) plus visibility. The disadvantage is that your boat will probably be crashing up and down in the swell all the while, which can make reboarding a distinctly dicey affair!

Despite, or perhaps because of, the exposed conditions the diving is excellent. There are great hard corals, including a dense patch of blue corals (*Heliopora* sp.) on the main reef slope, as well as some unusual sponges. Several different species of parrotfish, numerous jacks, emperorfish and goatfish, as well as many other smaller species, make this a delightful site for fish-watchers.

NELSON'S ISLAND

This is another exposed outpost, favoured by sea birds but rarely visited by people. Even on calm days the swell may prove too much to risk going ashore. But diving on the south side produces many delights. The wide, gently sloping reef is blanketed with the thickest growths of table corals than I have seen anywhere. Shallower than 10m (30ft), this gives way to flat, bare rock, evidence of the immense swells that can roll in even on this 'sheltered' side.

Heading towards deeper water, the rich coral slope ends abruptly at about 20 to 25m (65 to 80ft), where it meets the sand. There are a few caves along the boundary of the reef and the sand. These caves are home to a great diversity of nudibranchs, gobies and other tiny creatures. Big nurse sharks have also been seen here.

ABOVE *A pristine beach on a Chagos island.*
BELOW *A diver observes a thriving reef community.*
OPPOSITE TOP *The Chagos anemonefish (Amphiprion chagosensis) is, as its name suggests, endemic to the Chagos Archipelago.*
OPPOSITE BOTTOM *A tiny near-transparent commensal shrimp sheltering in an anemone.*

SRI LANKA

Charles Anderson

NEGOMBO THIRD REEF • HIKKADUWA • GREAT BASSES REEF

Sri Lanka does not feature on most people's wish list of must-see diving destinations. This is a shame, as not only does Sri Lanka boast marvellous scenery, fascinating monuments and friendly people, but it is also home to some extremely good Indian Ocean dive sites.

In the pioneering days of the 1950s and 1960s, Sri Lanka (then known as Ceylon) was the undisputed top dive destination of the Indian Ocean. Even today it offers some of the best diving in this region – you just have to know where to look.

In general the inshore dive sites tend to be rather murky and inshore reefs are often degraded. It is usually necessary to travel a little way offshore to find the best spots. This can make for some deep diving, although two of the top offshore dive sites selected here are both relatively shallow.

A very important point to keep in mind is that the island is strongly affected by the seasonal monsoons. That means that you have to plan your diving holidays carefully to get the best weather. Most dive centres on the popular southwest coast (for example at Bentota-Beruwela, Hikkaduwa, Unawatuna, Weligama and Dikwella) only operate during the northeast monsoon season, September/October to April/May. The diving off Negombo is best between January and April. The Great Basses Reef off the southeast coast is exposed to both monsoons, and is only accessible during the

months of March and April. If the political situation allows, there is some good diving off the east coast, notably at Trincomalee and nearby Nilaveli. For the east coast the best times for diving are during the latter part of the northeast and southwest seasons, from March to May (this is also the best time for whale-watching) and from August to November. During June/July strong offshore winds bring cold, murky, choppy water to this coast, so it is best avoided then.

It is important to realise that the ongoing civil unrest occurs mostly in the north and east. Colombo has had a few bomb attacks, but the southwest coast, with its many beach resorts, is safe. At the same time, because mass tourism has been disrupted by the unrest, there are some excellent travel bargains to be had.

While the country offers good diving, it would be a shame to visit it and not sample its many other attractions. The island is packed with places of interest, and is small enough to get around easily. The easiest way of travelling around is by cheap private taxi, with good public transport for the more adventurous. Top of the list of mainland attractions are the ancient monuments. The rock fortress at Sigiriya is definitely worth visiting, as is the ancient city of Polonnaruwa.

For wildlife enthusiasts, there is an abundance of bird, butterfly and plant species. Then there is the hill country, with its tea plantations, colonial-era hotels, bracing walks and stupendous

Opposite A Sri Lankan fishing outrigger beached at Negombo.
Top right Boats at Weligama, Sri Lanka.

CLIMATE
Hot, tropical. The northeast monsoon blows from October–April; the southwest monsoon from May/June–September. The first months of each monsoon brings strong winds and rain.

BEST TIME TO GO
Negombo: February/March; **Southwest coast:** October–March; **Great Basses Reef:** March/April; the **East coast:** April/May and August–October.

GETTING THERE
Flights to Katunayake International Airport near Negombo, an hour's drive from Colombo. Numerous scheduled and charter flights arrive from Europe, Asia and Australia. Divers with a lot of gear can hire a private taxi or minibus, with a driver.

WATER TEMPERATURE
Averages 26–31°C (78–88°F).

VISIBILITY
Often poor inshore. Negombo Third Reef, 20km (12 miles) offshore: 30m+ (100ft+).

QUALITY OF MARINE LIFE
Deeper reefs and those further offshore have good marine life. Species new to science are still being discovered regularly. There has been coral bleaching.

DEPTH OF DIVES
Inshore reefs: 2–15m (6–50ft). Further offshore: 15–40m+ (–130ft+).

SNORKELLING
At Unawatuna, Weligama and Dikwella.

NEGOMBO THIRD REEF

Negombo is not the most likely place to look for a top dive site. The waves crashing on the beach are muddy brown and not the least inviting. But do not be put off – you are in for a big surprise! This small coastal town north of Colombo is a bustling old market centre with an appealing, slightly down-at-heel atmosphere. The old fort, Dutch canal and vibrant fishing harbour add to its character. The beach north of town, with its strip of hotels, is the setting off point for this astonishingly good dive site.

Directly offshore, three great sandstone reefs run parallel to the coast. The First and Second Reefs offer reasonable diving, but the Third one out is in a class of its own. As you leave Negombo by boat and head out to the Third Reef, the water slowly changes from brown to green to blue. The coastline gradually recedes, becoming no more than a hazy pencil-line on the horizon. By the time you reach the Third Reef, 20km (12 miles) offshore, you are out of sight of land and in clear oceanic water.

The Third Reef is a low-lying rocky ridge, topped by massive coral heads, and dotted with smaller coral outcrops. It runs for several miles, and local dive operators have their own favourite spots. The reef does not break the surface, indeed few points of it are shallower than 18m (60ft), so due attention must be paid to bottom time, particularly on second dives.

The underwater scenery is not spectacular. Rather, the combination of relatively flat bottom and superb visibility imparts a magnificent feeling of space, of diving on a wide, open prairie. However, what makes this site so very appealing is the fish life. Great schools of snappers, goatfish and sweetlips hover in the shadows of the coral heads. Giant Napoleon wrasse and stingrays glide past and honeycomb moray eels peer from coral crevices. Smaller fish species are also present in abundance. Negombo may not be a top holiday destination, but its Third Reef is undoubtedly a top dive site.

An important consideration when diving from Negombo (and some other parts of Sri Lanka) is that it is affected by strong land breezes. During the day as the land heats up, air over the island rises, drawing in replacement air from the sea. The result is an onshore breeze, which can sometimes get very strong in the afternoon. During the night as the land cools, the wind dies. By morning the sea is often flat and calm. So it is best to be up early, get in two morning dives and be back for a late lunch. That also leaves the afternoon free for exploring the island's many other attractions.

HIKKADUWA

Hikkaduwa is the diving capital of Sri Lanka. A resort town on the southwest coast, it has far more dive operators than anywhere else on the island. The competition leads to rock-bottom prices, but also in some cases to rock-bottom service. In addition, many of the dives near Hikkaduwa are of mediocre quality, to put it politely, and are often afflicted by the poor visibility characteristic of many inshore sites. But check around for one of the better operators, who is prepared to go further offshore, and you can expect some good diving.

The *Conch*, an old steamer wreck north of the town, is a favourite local site. It is a bit close inshore to offer reliable visibility, so try to ascertain in advance if the water is clear enough to warrant a visit. The wreck is broken up, but the huge boilers and four-bladed propeller are still intact. The fish are well accustomed to visiting divers, and with clear water prove plentiful and obliging subjects for photographers.

Perhaps the best site regularly dived from Hikkaduwa is Malu Gala. This is a deep site, some way off shore, so it is not overdived and often has exceptional visibility. Malu Gala is a great rock pinnacle, rising up from about 40 to 20m (130 to 65ft).

LEFT   *A shoal of a species of grey sweetlips new to science* (Plectorhinchus *sp.*).

ABOVE   *Gardiner's butterflyfish* (Chaetodon gardineri) *prefer water deeper than 20m (65ft).*

The sides of the rock are home to numerous deep-water corals and other invertebrates (including this area's characteristic small blue sea fans), and to a host of reef fish. A safety stop on the mooring line at the end of the dive often provides a diverse parade of plankton to pass the time.

Hikkaduwa is also a convenient location from which to explore the other diving opportunities of the southwest coast. There are several dive operators scattered along the coast, most of whom have a couple of good sites in their repertoire. Try the shipwreck at Dikwella, Monolith Rock near Weligama, and Beruwela's Mada Gala.

GREAT BASSES REEF

Off the southeast coast of Sri Lanka, exposed to the full force of both monsoons, is the rocky outcrop known as Great Basses Reef. The name Basses derives from the word *baixos*, meaning reef, bestowed by early Portuguese navigators. This is an inhospitable place, lashed by storms and huge waves for most of the year. It has been a source of danger for ships throughout the ages, as several shipwrecks attest. Because of this danger a lighthouse was installed by the colonial British government during the 1860s, and it still provides a beacon for the shipping that passes just offshore.

The diving on the inside of the reef is, frankly, a trifle tame. The flat sandstone bottom slopes gently down to the sand at about 12m (40ft). In the shadow of the lighthouse, the anchors and jumbled remains of the 'soda wreck' – so-called after its 150-year-old cargo of pop bottles – provides an interesting potter (don't forget that it is prohibited to remove anything from any wreck here). But the clear water and abundant fish hint at Great Basses' true attraction. That is the outer side of the reef, where the sandstone has been sculpted into grotesque formations and remarkably shaped passageways. Here, in the clearest of water and accompanied by squadrons of fish, the diver can explore convoluted swim-throughs, aided by the constant

RIGHT *A diver swims alongside a school of goatfish* (Mullidae) *and snappers* (Lutjanidae) *on Negombo Third Reef. Some 20km (12 miles) offshore, this reef offers great fish-viewing opportunities in clear oceanic waters.*

to-and-fro of the ocean surge. Sunlight streaming through the reef adds to the allure. With maximum depths in the range of 12 to 14m (40 to 46ft), extended dive·times are the norm.

The world-class quality of the diving at Great Basses was first reported by Arthur C Clarke, the author and science-fiction guru who is a long-term resident of Sri Lanka. His team discovered the wreck of a treasure ship on the reef in 1961.

Because of its exposed position, Great Basses is only accessible for diving during the March/April period, between the monsoons. Because of its remoteness, off the Yala National Park, and miles from the nearest dive centre, just getting to the reef is always a major undertaking. However, the difficulties of getting there are more than compensated for by the satisfaction of reaching and diving this exceptional site.

ABOVE *The relatively common honeycomb moray eel* (Gymnothorax favagineus) *feeds on smaller reef fish.* BOTTOM (left to right) *A cleaner shrimp; a feather star; and vivid soft corals at Hikkaduwa.*

OPPOSITE (left, top to bottom) Glossodoris *sp. nudibranchs from Western Australia;* Phyllidia ocellata *from the Indo-Pacific;* Flabellina rubrolineata, *from South Australia;* (right) Risbecia pulchells *from the Red Sea.*

NUDIBRANCHS

Nudibranchs are commonly known as sea slugs. This un-prepossessing name refers to some of the most exuberantly colourful and beautiful of all reef inhabitants.

Like their distant relatives, the land slugs, sea slugs are snails that have lost their shells. This may be because their distant ancestors were burrowers, and a shell would have have hindered efficient burrowing. In sea snails, the gills are typically tucked away under the shell. With the loss of the shell, the gills of sea slugs are exposed — hence the scientific name nudibranch (or 'naked gill'). In many nudibranchs, such as Chromodoris sea slugs, the gills are fully exposed as a feathery rosette on the back. In Phyllidia

sea slugs the gills are tucked away underneath a fold on one side of the body, so paradoxically these are hidden-gilled naked-gilled animals. In yet other forms, for example Flabellina, there are no gills at all, but a series of projections, or cerata, on the back. These cerata increase the surface area of these nudibranchs to such an extent that sufficient oxygen exchange occurs without the need for gills.

With the loss of their protective shells, nudibranchs have developed a number of ingenious strategies for escaping predation. The simplest of all is camouflage, and many sea slugs are almost impossible to see when sitting on their chosen food. Other nudibranchs feed on anemones and

similar animals with stinging cells. They absorb the stinging cells, pass them unfired into their cerata, and recycle them for use against their own would-be predators. Still other nudibranchs are poisonous or foul tasting, and advertise this with loud colours.

A major problem for the small, slow-moving nudibranchs is finding a mate in the vastness of a reef. Thus all nudibranchs are hermaphrodites (each individual having the reproductive organs of both sexes). So whenever two nudibranchs meet they are able to mate. Eggs are laid in mucous sheets, which take the form of attractive spiral ribbons or long, beaded strings.

EASTERN INDIAN OCEAN

MYANMAR

Paul Lees

MERGUI ARCHIPELAGO

The Mergui Archipelago is one of the most charming island groups in all of Southeast Asia. Comprising 804 islands, islets and rocky knolls, it covers a total area of 16,363km² (6,316 sq. miles), spanning from Tavoy Island in the north down to Myanmar's southern border with Thailand.

The largest island in the chain, King Island, is cultivated by a mixture of Bamas and Karen nationals. Of the other larger islands Kisseraing and Sellore are also inhabited, but only during the harsher monsoon months when nomadic sea gypsies referred to as Mokens use them for shelter.

The islands' topographies are unusually diverse; heavily-pitted limestone karsts contrast with white powdery beaches such as those fringing Great Western Torres and Lampi Island. Other landmasses range from tiny outcrops barely punctuating the ocean's surface, to heavily forested elevations.

In the north, the small port of Mergui remains as industrious today as it has been for the last three centuries. Located on Mergui Island, it welcomes the many boats that come in to offload cargos or replenish supplies. Today, however, visitors to the region can enjoy a more secure passage than their predecessors could hope to expect, when acts of piracy were rampant and many vessels were captured by pirates waiting in concealed bays on the outer western approaches to the port.

The archipelago's waters were re-opened to outsiders for the first time in 50 years in January 1997, and while the area is now safely accessible, much of what lies below the surface remains a mystery. Myanmar has as yet no diving services of its own, but a number of the more established operators based in neighbouring Thailand now schedule regular live-aboard excursions into the area. To date, their diving experiences have been very positive.

The underwater terrain here tends to be more rugged than that found in the more southern regions of the Andaman Sea. For instance, the soft corals occur in more compact and sheltered areas and are not as widespread as they are further south.

A major attraction is diving with sharks, and there are a lot of them, in both quantity and variety! These include grey and black and whitetip reef, nurse, and even silvertip sharks. Big fish include rays and a wealth of pelagics such as rainbow runners, tuna, mackerel, trevally, jacks and barracuda.

The excitement created by the quantity and variety of open ocean fish at sites such as Black Rock and the Burma Banks is quite indescribable, and on occasion further amplified by the presence of whale sharks and various oceanic sharks.

On a smaller, less animated scale a cornucopia of smaller reef creatures provide excellent photographic opportunities, particularly in the deeper reef zones where huge gorgonian sea fans provide both sanctuary and hunting grounds for smaller members of the reef community.

CLIMATE

In the dry season (October–May) conditions are hot and sunny, and the seas calm.

BEST TIME TO GO

The dry season. However, diving expeditions to the southern islands of the Mergui Archipelago can run all year round.

GETTING THERE

Trips depart from the port of Kaw Thaung on Victoria Point, which can be reached from the town of Ranong on Thailand's west coast. You can fly directly to Ranong from Bangkok. The flight time is 80 minutes. You can also drive to Ranong from Phuket Island, in about four hours.

WATER TEMPERATURE

Averages in excess of 28°C (82°F).

VISIBILITY

Good in the dry season, with a range of anything from 5–40m (16–130ft).

QUALITY OF MARINE LIFE

Corals and reef fish abound, but the focus here falls on both larger visitors, with examples being found in deeper waters, and a profusion of minute creatures at all depths.

DEPTH OF DIVES

Best below 15m (50ft).

PRACTICALITIES

There are no local operators. Equipment is available on Koh Phuket as are the nearest recompression facilities. A permit is required, which must be paid for in US$. It is paid to the dive operator, before departure.

BLACK ROCK

About halfway north along the Mergui Archipelago, a single craggy outcrop stands proud of the water by some 20m (65ft), spreading more than five times that from east to west. The southern side of the rock drops to varying depths and at different inclines; in places it is sheer, in others it climbs down ledges and over enormous boulders.

The southwestern apex of the site features a series of gently sloping granite plateaus, positioned slightly away from the main rock. Their surfaces are often almost completely obscured by pink and white bushes of soft corals, among which a multitude of bearded scorpionfish and common reef octopuses lie incognito. In fact I have never seen as many of these creatures in one place anywhere else in the world. On a smaller scale, but with a slightly more obvious presence, a great many tiny hawkfish and blennies flit around nervously, obviously disturbed by the intrusion of divers into their domain.

The far side of these plateaus drops to in excess of 40m (130ft), and these deeper waters are one of the preferred locations for spotting grey reef sharks as they circle around, gradually approaching a wide gully that separates this colourful area from the main rocky structure. On the odd occasion other visiting sharks also grace the waters with their presence, as does the enormous whale shark.

A prolific amount of marine life frequents not only the surfaces of the main structure but also its immediate environs. Close scrutiny will reveal the likes of almost transparent cleaner shrimps, minute coral snails and crinoid crabs, surreal nudibranchs and a collection of well camouflaged cephalopods with their colorations adjusted to blend in with their backgrounds.

The layout of the northern reef differs quite dramatically in that it descends somewhat more gradually over a jumble of rocks of varying sizes to a depth of around 30m (100ft). Here the rocks meet the sandy sea bed, which slopes yet more gradually downwards. Scattered over this slope are a series of small boulders, the larger of which have individual reef communities of their own.

The majority of the reef inhabitants found around these rocky slopes are those typically found in areas such as this; black-banded sea kraits and a variety of moray eels meander around

the narrow gaps in search of food and employ the many dark recesses as lairs and places to be tended to by cleaning invertebrates.

Both benthic (bottom-dwelling) and pelagic fish are prolific all around this site, with bluering and emperor angelfish adding splashes of colour to the rocks. A curtain of schooling batfish act as a living blind to incoming predators, such as barracuda and cobia.

At night and in the right conditions, diving here can be extremely exciting, although one does have to remain closer to the rock than in the daylight hours as there are always a couple of curious sharks to be wary of!

WESTERN ROCKY

This is the southernmost of the current dive destinations, and is generally visited either on the way to, or back from, the Burma Banks. It lies some 82km (50 miles) southwest of the departure point, Kaw Thaung on Victoria Point. The best way to describe the surface topography is as a collection of rocky pillars of varying sizes, above which a family of white-bellied sea eagles nest. This site is not typical to the area in that the reefs are separated; either to individually fringe the larger of the outcrops or to connect the adjoining smaller ones. Therefore even a couple of dives at this diverse site are really insufficient to cover it in its entirety.

The biggest of the rocky structures features a couple of caves, the largest of which has an entrance in the southern wall right next to a splendid rocky archway covered in soft corals. The entrance can be found at around 20m (65ft) and its opening continues right through the rock as a tunnel with its heavily-pitted walls and ceiling being laden with painted rock lobsters, who seek refuge in the many dark crevices. The eyes of these armoured invertebrates brightly reflect the beams of light emitted by necessary torches.

After a relatively short distance the tunnel dips to the right, into a small bowl formation; this on occasion hosts an irritable 2m (6ft) nurse shark. Continuing through the tunnel offers a choice of two exits; with the larger and more preferred one being to the right. There is often no choice as to which to use, however, as aside from the fact that the other exit is a lot smaller, it is usually blocked by a number of nurse sharks.

The other cave in the western face is somewhat smaller and not as exciting. However, the immediate surrounds of its entrance mark out an area host to three frogfish, as well as lionfish, scorpionfish and stonefish, and is well worth a look.

There is a great range of marine life around the rocky walls and reefs around this site as well as further afield, both in and around the varying structures in the sea bed. On the rocks, black-banded sea kraits twist by sea anemones tended by porcelain crabs, shrimps and a selection of anemonefish, while deeper down tiger cowries explore gorgonian sea fans. In the wide ravines below, among the coral substrate sea bed, ribbon eels mingle with burrowing gobies and pistol shrimps, while above them groups of amorous cuttlefish search for partners. Away from the reef action grey, blacktip and whitetip reef sharks patrol along an abrupt step in the sandy sea bed, from 26 to 34m (85 to 112ft) to the west of the larger reef.

OPPOSITE TOP *Black Rock stands 20m (65ft) above the surface of the water.*
OPPOSITE BOTTOM *A common reef octopus (Octopus cyanea) awaits its prey on top of a coral mound.*
RIGHT *Although they occur in more localized, smaller patches than they do further south in the Andaman Sea, this region has beautiful soft corals.*

BURMA BANKS

These submerged seamounts, collectively referred to as the Burma Banks, lie 60km (37 miles) to the west of Western Rocky. They project irregularly from the sea bed, rising from a depth of 300m (1000ft) to around 15m (50ft); there are no land references to pinpoint their actual whereabouts so their exact location is only determined with the aid of navigational equipment.

These sites were first visited in 1990 and then closed down by the authorities soon afterwards. Today they are again accessible, and are included as part of Mergui Archipelago excursions. There are four known banks – Rainbow, Roe, Big and Silvertip – the first three are only dived occasionally and it is the easternmost bank, Silvertip, which is the most frequently visited.

SILVERTIP BANK

Rocky alleyways, grottos and small tunnels stand proud of an otherwise rugged current-dictated terrain of fragmented coral substrate, which adds to the main attraction of this site – sharks, and plenty of them, hence the name. Some operators will allow divers the opportunity of experiencing shark feeding, induced or otherwise. This practice obviously increases shark presence, which in turn adds a certain element of excitement, whether or not this practice has a long term effect on the animals' behaviour remains to be seen, particularly in maturing juveniles.

At the top end of the shark activity are silvertip sharks, and on occasion, oceanic whitetip sharks, the odd hammerhead and even tiger sharks. Further down the ladder there are small gatherings of tawny nurse sharks swimming around in nose-to-tail chain-like formations. And last but not least, are the occasional visiting whale sharks, and even manta and eagle rays.

LEFT *Divers admire a large sea fan through a cloud of iridescent fish. Feather stars have used the sea fan as a substrate from which to reach out into the current.*
ABOVE *The extravagantly beautiful red-belted anthia* (Pseudanthias rubrizonatus).

This terrain is littered with the more sturdy of coral formations such as solid mounds of lesser star and brain corals, and the thicker members of branching corals, for instance staghorn, whose branches are navigated by a selection of damselfish and chromis.

On a larger scale are closely scattered groups of boulders and rocks with narrow interconnecting gullies and canyons obscured by gorgonian sea fans and stinging hydroids. Ordinarily these are wide enough for divers to pass through but the odd section still serves as a secure shark-watching station. The highest proportion of soft corals here are found clinging to the sheltered parts of rocky structures, mainly due to the fact that ripping currents, particularly during the monsoon seasons, have carried any more exposed specimens into the abyss.

The fish life here is also pretty good, and those not completely distracted by the members of the shark family will notice a number of different families of fish divisible into numerous groups. There are Indian Ocean bird wrasse and crescent wrasse; spadefish (batfish) including longfin spadefish; there are red snappers, Indian and titan triggerfish; bullethead and bumphead parrotfish; emperor and bluering angelfish; and harlequin and Oriental sweetlips.

Unfortunately, there are patches of coral bleaching caused by the 1997–98 El Niño phenomenon, but the damage is minimal and not every species has suffered. Your attention is better directed at the multitude of crinoids on the healthy survivors.

ABOVE LEFT *A false clownfish* (Amphiprion ocellaris) *tends to its host, a magnificent sea anemone.*
ABOVE *Christmas tree worms* (Spirobranchus giganteus).
BELOW *Common nurse sharks* (Nebrius ferrugineus) *rest in caves during the day. They are nocturnal feeders.*

THAILAND

Paul Lees

KOH PHUKET · MU KOH SURIN · MU KOH SIMILAN · KOH PHI PHI · KOH LANTA

The Kingdom of Thailand occupies the very heart of Southeast Asia, an ideal location for both international trading and as a hub for recreational travel throughout the region. The country covers an area of around 49,350km² (190,500 sq. miles) with a population topping the 58 million mark, most of whom reside in the capital city, Bangkok.

Thailand is bordered by Malaysia in the south, Myanmar (formerly Burma) to the west, Laos to the north and northeast, and Cambodia to the east.

Whereas the country's northern region is covered with undulating hills and extensive mountainous terrain, the south is adorned with splendid palm-fringed tropical islands and glorious mainland beaches. The largest and best known of the islands (*koh* means island in Thai), Koh Phuket, is an established international tourist destination, and a steady growth of visitors has slowly resulted in tourist services spreading further afield to nearby island groups. Koh Phuket is the favoured take-off point for Thailand's many excellent dive sites.

Of the sites visited on live-aboard excursions, the waters around Mu Koh (meaning island group) Surin house the oldest and most developed corals around the country, accompanied by a prolific diversity and quantity of marine life. Further south, the Similan islands are renowned as one of the world's top dive sites, with spectacular granite topside landscapes and breathtaking underwater scenery.

A number of islands nearer Phuket are now enjoying a brisk tourist trade. To the east the Koh Phi Phi group have increased their available services from basic thatched huts to include a range of air-conditioned accommodations, and also now have restaurants and tourist services. Further south, the world-class beaches of Krabi Province are now being developed in a similar vein.

Still further south, the more laid-back island of Koh Lanta Yai maintains its undeveloped beaches and a more basic line of accommodation.

Heading down from Koh Lanta, towards Malaysia, and also forming part of the Koh Lanta Marine National Park, Hin Daeng and Hin Mouang are great dive locations with tremendous coral drop-offs, soft corals and diverse marine life in both shallow and deep water.

The widespread distribution of dive services allows the country to offer a more than adequate selection and variety of exhilarating destinations, all divable either as daily or multi-day live-aboard excursions. Breathtaking reef formations of both hard and soft corals await divers in the form of fringing reefs, sheer walls and even on the odd sunken vessel.

Also attracted to these sites are prolific schools of open ocean fish and marine mammals in search of nutrition and shelter. Whale sharks and manta rays are established seasonal visitors.

Opposite The narrow isthmus of Koh Phi Phi Don is the main area for accommodation on the island.
Top right KorLae fishing boats have been handpainted for generations, each continuing a distinct family style.

CLIMATE
During the dry season (October–May), the area experiences hot and sunny conditions and the seas are generally calm.

BEST TIME TO GO
The dry season when water temperatures range from 27–31°C (80.6–88°F).

GETTING THERE
Phuket International Airport can be reached directly from a number of regional destinations. Fourteen domestic flights depart Bangkok airport bound for Phuket every day. The flight time is 75 minutes. In Phuket it is necessary to transfer by taxi or air-conditioned minibus to your live-aboard operator.

WATER TEMPERATURE
Averages in excess of 28°C (82°F).

VISIBILITY
Good in the dry season with a range of anything from 5–40m (16–130ft).

DEPTH OF DIVES
From 3m (10ft) to 40m+ (130ft+).

SNORKELLING
Many areas have snorkelling sites, mostly accessed from boats.

PRACTICALITIES
Dive operators concentrate mostly around the PADI agency, ranging from small personal one-man concerns up to five-star facilities. Dive trips and education are obtainable on arrival, but it is better to prebook. The nearest recompression facilities are located on Koh Phuket.

KOH PHUKET

Koh Phuket's west coast is broken by a number of beaches, which are the main tourist centres. All dive services are on offer, including dive education up to and including instructor, daily diving trips to the top sites within easy reach of the island, and regularly scheduled multi-day live-aboard excursions to all of the world-class destinations further afield. Phuket serves as the main base for accessing sites around the Andaman Sea. Sites such as the Burma Banks, Koh Phi Phi, Mu Koh Surin and Mu Koh Similan, and even those south of Koh Lanta are all served by the dive centres and operators on this island.

Local diving is scheduled weekly, and specific sites are visited on set days, allowing divers to plan their own schedules. The timetables differ between the centres, which helps in minimizing the number of boats and divers at any one site at any given time. Divers generally depart from the dive centres, or are picked up at their resort at around 08:00. Dive boats leave from Chalong Bay at the southern end of the island, and they return here between 16:00 and 18.00. The larger, more established operators serve all of the offshore dive sites southeast of Koh Phuket on board fully equipped dive boats.

The diving off the island's southwest coast is by no means world-class. Visibility around these sites can be limited as a result of heavy silting. Better conditions are to be found to the south of the island around the offshore outcrops and islands. Here currents carry away any quantities of algae or silt, replacing them with clearer waters (and allowing a more abundant coral growth), with visibility often in excess of 30m (100ft).

The general health and representation of corals is both diverse and plentiful, with a range in hues of soft corals gracing numerous sites; some of which are deep and can have ripping currents, rendering them more suitable for experienced divers. Large pelagics are often present, and there is a good selection of crustaceans, other invertebrates and reef fish.

There are a number of destinations to the southeast of Koh Phuket that are well worth visiting, and perhaps the pick of these is Shark Point Marine Sanctuary, closely followed by the waters surrounding Koh Phi Phi some way further south.

SHARK POINT MARINE SANCTUARY

In 1992 two established and popular diving sites, Shark Point and Anemone Reef, were designated as a protected marine sanctuary. In 1997, as a result of a collision, a third site was added to the list – the *King Cruiser* car ferry.

SHARK POINT

Hin Musang, locally referred to as Shark Point, consists of three submerged pinnacles lying north–south, which between them have a particularly high proportion of both hard and soft corals at all depths.

All manner of reef residents animate the otherwise fixed patterns of colour. Leopard sharks are the main attraction here, and many a diver has had the wonderful experience of observing this harmless bottom-feeder at close quarters.

On a smaller scale, Hin Musang features numerous cleaning stations hosted by a multitude of cleaner fish and invertebrates. Regular customers at these cleaning stations include a variety of snappers, jacks, trevally, mackerel and even the occasional barracuda.

Although the diving all around this popular site is very impressive, the highest concentration of

marine life is to be found at the southernmost pinnacle. This is a community all on its own, with pipefish, wrasse, damselfish, parrotfish and a host of cephalopods.

ANEMONE REEF

The second protected site is a completely submerged pinnacle referred to as Anemone Reef. The shallowest part sits a mere 7m (23ft) below the water's surface and is literally covered in sea anemones hosting numerous species of clownfish.

OPPOSITE TOP *Nai Harn Beach on Koh Phuket. The island is known both for good diving and watersports, and for the beautiful beaches on its western coastline.*
OPPOSITE BOTTOM *Although it may look dangerous, the leopard shark* (Stegastoma fasciatum) *is actually a docile and harmless bottom-feeder.*
ABOVE *Sea anemones festoon the reefscape at Anemone Reef, one of three protected sites forming the Shark Point Marine Sanctuary, southeast of Phuket Island.*

Closer inspection reveals even more symbiotic residents; tiny anemone crabs and transparent cleaner shrimps – only visible by their translucent internal organs. Below these, enormous healthy gorgonian sea fans form a dramatic backdrop to hovering prides of Indian lionfish and large clusters of radiant soft corals.

The pinnacle is not, as is the case with other obstructions in these waters, without its share of ledges and crevices, and divers visiting this monolith will be amazed at the selection of moray eels hiding there.

The pinnacle is now only half its former size (see below), but the marine life has stayed and relocated. Since the ferry accident in 1997 the marine life throughout this site has seemingly increased two-fold.

KING CRUISER CAR FERRY

On May 4th 1997 the *King Cruiser*, a car ferry operating between Koh Phuket and the Phi Phi islands, bottomed on Anemone Reef – splitting the

pinnacle in two. The impact of the collision also tore a large hole in the vessel's hull, and 17 minutes later it was on the sea bed.

The *King Cruiser* now sits on the bottom in 32m (105ft) of water. The structure has attracted a high diversity of marine life and the formation of an artificial reef is well under way. Numerous invertebrates have taken to sheltering beneath small sheets of peeling paint, and morays lie in wait under rows of seats – now acting as lairs. Around the barnacle-encrusted frame are schools of juvenile reef fish that seemingly increase in size and number with every visit.

Daylight penetrates most areas of the wreck, but there are still a number of areas that would certainly be better explored with the aid of a torch. In addition to this, divers intending to explore the interior should be aware that some areas of the ferry have collapsed ceilings, which have the potential to fall even further. As is the case with most wrecks, it is best to dive the wreck of the *King Cruiser* at slack tide.

MU KOH SURIN

This island group is located in the Andaman Sea 60km (37 miles) due west of the town of Koraburi, Phang Na Province, and the same distance northeast of Mu Koh Similan, with the Myanmar border only a few kilometres to the north. The area was designated the country's 29th Marine National Park in 1981, and consists of five granite islands and two rocky outcrops covering 135km² (52 sq. miles), 76 per cent of which is water.

The largest island, Koh Surin Nua, has an area of 18km² (7 sq. miles), and its highest point is 240m (790ft) above sea level. To the immediate southwest lies Koh Surin Tai – covering 12km² (4.6 sq. miles) – which stands slightly proud of its neighbour with its highest point being 350m (1150ft) above sea level.

These, the two largest islands, are covered with primary evergreen forest, the supporting canopies of which average a height of 32m (105ft). The island also has a sprinkling of mangrove forests around its southeastern and eastern coastlines. This floral diversity has attracted a wide spectrum

of wildlife, although due to the distance from the mainland the selection is restricted to somewhat smaller creatures. lesser mouse deer, endemic grey-bellied squirrels, and island flying foxes all favour the inaccessible areas of forest, whereas crab-eating macaques and Malayan flying lemurs are often seen foraging about the coastal areas, particularly around the accommodation facilities at the park headquarters. There are more than 80 bird species here, including collared kingfishers, Nicobar pigeons, wreathed hornbills, greater racket-tailed drongos, Abbott's babbler, white-bellied sea eagles and Brahminy kites.

There are only three locations inhabited by humans on the island; the park headquarters on the west coast, a small fishing community on the southern coast, and a Chao Ley village also on the southern coast. There is another Chao Ley village across the sound, on the adjacent beach on

Koh Surin Tai. These nomadic fishermen originate from Indonesia, but now temporarily shelter on a few of the islands in the Andaman Sea.

The coral reefs around these two Surin islands are renowned as being the most established in Thai waters, are also noted for the high diversity of species, and feature the widest reef flats in the region. These reefs have been found to date back to the last ice age, a fact proven by the presence of blue holes – a phenomenon caused by collapsing ice. This is the only location in Thailand where this is evident. During 1998 a request was issued for the area to be listed as a World Heritage Site.

As far as specific underwater locations are concerned, there are a number to which scuba diving is suited. Preferred destinations follow fringing reefs or circumnavigate small islets, rocky outcrops and submerged pinnacles. The majority of underwater attractions fringing the larger islands are good for snorkelling, making them accessible to divers of all levels. Park officials registered more than 53,000 guests snorkelling the reefs as long ago as 1994, and numbers have increased since then.

KOH SURIN NUA

Koh Surin Nua offers a handful of interesting locations, and Mai Ngam on its west coast is one of the best places to catch glimpses of green and hawksbill turtles as they come ashore to begin the arduous task of laying their eggs. On the east coast Mae Yai and Chon kar feature the largest reefs in the park. The reef flat extends for over 1km (0.6 miles) in places. Between these two areas, enormous sea fans and coral bombies (heads) grace the deeper waters.

To the northeast, Koh Chi is among the classic locations to observe large visiting pelagics such as great barracuda, dogtooth tuna, threadfin trevally, and big-eye jacks. It is also good for seeing turtles on their way to and from Koh Surin Nua, including the rarely seen leatherback.

TOP LEFT *A solitary longfin bannerfish* (Heniochus acuminatus) *swims past an array of corals and reef fish in the Mu Koh Surin Marine National Park.*
ABOVE *A black boxfish* (Ostracion meleagris).

Tables of staghorn corals dominate the shallower sections of the reef, and their associated marine life includes whitetip reef sharks. Smaller, more colourful residents include blue-spotted ribbontail stingrays, powder-blue surgeons, brown tangs, bullethead parrotfish and a variety of wrasse. Snorkellers can enjoy the waters around the rocks' perimeters, where they can observe a selection of table corals and rocks highlighted by christmas-tree worms and feather stars, along with a selection of bivalves. There are also patches of gigantic and magnificent sea anemones hosting anemonefish and a range of symbiotic invertebrates. To the west, Hin Rap shares similar underwater features with the added bonus of whale sharks.

KOH SURIN TAI

Of the Koh Surin Tai sites, Turtle Ledge is certainly the best. The higher portions of the reef slope have numerous gardens of sea anemones, the majority of which host false clown anemonefish. Clusters of staghorn corals climb over specimens of the largest of the giant clam family, some spanning 137cm (54in). The site acquired its name from the frequent sightings of turtles, in particular the hawksbill, but there are many other visitors, including big schools of titan triggerfish, snappers and sweetlips.

Hin Tacksin, off the southern tip of the island, is a collection of submerged rocks richly highlighted by red and purple soft corals. At the reef at Koh

---

Torinla 248 species of marine life have been identified to date, 15 of which are different species of sea slug. In the eastern area there is a small garden of magnificent sea anemones hosting pink skunk and Clark's anemonefish. Coral groupers shelter beneath many fine flower corals, and there are also many members of the chromis family darting among wide tables of staghorns. Many shelves of rocks appear at varying depths, all with different features. The shallower ones host hermit crabs, jewel-box urchins and cleaner shrimps, and are rich in colourful Bennett's feather stars.

Away from the reef, the adjoining sandy plains are scattered with mushroom corals and a number of Graeffe's and black sea cucumbers.

RICHELIEU ROCK

Fourteen kilometres (8.7 miles) east of the two Surin Islands lies the whale shark 'magnet' of Richelieu Rock. There are also a multitude of other spectacular attractions, both resident and visiting, around this five-pronged, submerged pinnacle.

The three southern pinnacles sit in 22m (72ft) and feature large numbers of orange gorgonian sea fans, immediately beneath many hues of soft corals. Their rocky surfaces are host to bearded scorpionfish, stonefish, moray eels, long-spined sea urchins, shrimps, crabs and surreal nudibranchs. The radiant hermetypic corals also support a wide diversity of marine life, and residents include schooling bannerfish, blackspot and humpback snappers, Indian and spotfin lionfish, Moorish idols and titan triggerfish. Close inspection of the rocks reveals all sorts of inhabitants displaying interesting interactions; gardens of sea anemones are hosts to a variety of anemonefish, anemone shrimps and crabs.

As this location is the only food source in the immediate area, it is a first-class site for spotting large pelagics, with plenty of species to choose from. Rainbow runners; chevron, great and yellowtail barracuda; trevally; tuna and jacks are common.

The sea bed here consists of sand mixed with fragmented coral substrate, and is home to a variety of molluscs (including large squid and octopuses) and gastropods. The latter include Lister's conch, textile cone and mitre shells. There is a resident family of white-spotted shovelnose rays, with their half-shark, half-ray bodies.

Top *A tiny harlequin shrimp* (Hymenocera picta) *eating a sea star many times its size.*

Right *Beautiful red soft corals adorn a sloping drop-off. These are typical of Hin Tacksin, off Koh Surin Tai.*

MU KOH SIMILAN

There are two legends that suggest how this archipelago of nine forested, granite retreats received their collective title. The first states that the Similans were named, along with several other sanctuaries in the Andaman Sea, after young village maidens who were presented as gifts to rich European settlers in exchange for varying amounts of financial support. The second, more popular explanation, states that the name is derived from the Malay word *sembilan*, which translates as the number nine.

This, Thailand's most talked about diving destination, rises above the Andaman Sea 92km (57 miles) northwest of Koh Phuket, and was declared a Marine National Park in 1982. The surrounding 130km² (50 sq. miles) of ocean were also included within the park. With the exception of the unnamed island Number Five, they are individually labelled with both names and numbers, ascending northwards. To enforce the designation of Marine National Park the Royal Forestry Department installed two park offices and the duty rangers remain as the only permanent residents on any of the islands, although the Royal Thai Navy temporarily act as both nanny and protector for a turtle rehabilitation project on Koh Huyong.

The topography of the islands' east and west coasts differs, in that the former have been shaped by kinder weather conditions. These more sheltered coastlines feature sandy beaches underlined by gently sloping reefs, whereas the more exposed west coasts feature stacks of hard, weather-beaten boulders rising from the sea bed, crowned by leaning trees forced over by the harsh southwesterly monsoon winds.

These configurations continue beneath the waterline. The eastern reefs feature gentle slopes of mostly hard corals, although there is a healthy presence of soft corals on the lower slopes, and solitary boulders in the deeper waters. The sheer magnificence and colours of both these reefs is really quite awe-inspiring.

The western coastlines are equally splendid, as they are typified by giant boulders tumbling down to the sea bed. Adjoining gaps are swept free of sand and coral fragments by strong currents during the harsher months, which clear the way for exciting tunnels, arches, caverns and crevices, all waiting to be explored – whereas other more scattered pinnacles and plateaus act as submerged auditoriums for fans of pelagic species.

An immense diversity of marine life enjoys these waters. There are more than 200 recorded species of hard corals alone, along with a high presence and variety of soft corals. The surrounding water clarity is also very high, with visibility frequently topping the 30m (100ft) mark. There is, however, a drop in visibility during the country's hottest month of March, when a rise in the water temperature results in a plankton bloom. This in turn increases the spectrum of marine life, particularly the pelagic visitors – here tuna, barracuda, jacks and trevally are accompanied by manta and eagle rays and the occasional whale shark.

There is world-class diving to be found all around the archipelago, and each established dive site has its outstanding points – a brief outline of which follows, beginning off the northwest coast of Koh Bangu, Island Nine.

CHRISTMAS POINT

Boulders of various shapes and sizes fringe the island's northern shoreline in depths averaging 25m (82ft). These tend to increase in size and depth towards the north, their upper slopes punctuated by soft corals which are, due to their shallow positions, erratically highlighted by dancing rays of sunlight refracted through the surface. The corals also fringe small rocky overhangs with large pockets of trapped air around their parabolic ceilings. There are no corals in these as they would simply suffocate, but lionfish seem to be curiously drawn to admire themselves in the reflective air pockets.

Wide areas in-between the jumble of rocks are shared by various hard corals, the most common being broad plate corals. The narrow gaps and steps between them serve as cleaning stations for giant morays, who are tended to by shrimps. Oriental

sweetlips enjoy a similar service from cleanerfish – V-shaped squadrons can be seen patiently awaiting their turn in the surrounding waters.

The western quadrant of the site differs in that a couple of wedge-shaped archways lead through an enormous rocky centrepiece. Passing through these dramatically alters the seascape, and they also act as handy escape routes if the current suddenly picks up, which tends to happen here.

FANTASEA REEF

A matrix of submerged boulders rise from the sea bed around 50m (164ft) from the northwestern coastline of Koh Similan, spreading out towards the west. This scattered collection of plateaus actually has several names, the most common of which is Fantasea Reef.

Extensive rocky mounds are interconnected by wide gulleys with other solitary pinnacles marking out the site's perimeter. The higher rocky platforms sit 14m (46ft) below the surface, while others drop to beyond 40m (130ft). Large crevices split the otherwise unbroken surfaces in leaf-vein formations, the main arteries of which are flanked by impressive gorgonians. The adjoining and tighter thoroughfares are used as ambushes and lairs for a variety of fish and moray eels.

OPPOSITE A diver explores a reefscape covered in soft corals and gorgonians at Fantasea Reef in Mu Koh Similan Marine National Park.

TOP Donald Duck Bay on the west coast of Koh Similan, Island Number Eight.

RIGHT A diminutive goby (Eviota sp.) resting among coral polyps.

The diversity of marine life in every part of this site is outstanding. A variety of triggerfish mingle with schools of parrotfish, coral groupers, lionfish and sweetlips. These move against a backdrop of sea fans, sponges, feather stars and soft corals. The bottom composition between them is fragmented coral substrate – peer hard into it as this is the home of the tiny but magnificent ribbon eel, and both the blue-bodied adult males and black juveniles are frequently sighted. The best way to locate these eels is to look out for decorated dartfish (or purple fire gobies) that hover slightly above the bottom; the eels are never far away.

BEACON REEF

Fringing the eastern coast of Koh Similan is Beacon Reef, the longest continual coral structure in the island group. The reef flat sits in just more than 5m (16ft) of water, and is comprised of many small boulders of brain corals interspersed with clusters of staghorn. These are all rich with a variety of colourful reef fish including wrasse, damselfish, parrotfish and surgeonfish.

The coral formations remain constant over the southern section of the reef, with specimens increasing in size with depth on the reef slopes. Hard leaf corals such as lettuce corals mix with a variety of horizontal plate corals. The fish life is similar to that found in the shallower waters, although the quantity and species count is larger. It is not uncommon to see small whitetip reef sharks swagger by in the greater depths, where there is a chain of coral heads covered in soft corals, their colourful presence further enriched by orange and blue encrusting sponges and multicoloured feather stars.

The reef ends off the southern tip of the island, and this area has been singled out as Beacon Point. It is one of the most favourable points in the Similans for observing stingrays, and there have been more encounters with manta and eagle rays here than anywhere else in the park.

ELEPHANT HEAD ROCK

To the immediate southwest of Koh Similan, Elephant Head Rock is a small gathering of weatherbeaten boulders that break the surface, the larger and southernmost of which resembles a swimming elephant's head.

The underwater terrain here is breathtaking; the dive takes you around massive sunken boulders, some touching to form frames measuring more than 30m (100ft) across, with narrow gaps creating daring swim-throughs.

The sea bed falls to beyond 30m (100ft) to the east of the main structure. Heading in this direction takes you past smaller boulders topped in places with spreading stands of staghorn corals. Numbers of patrolling reef sharks including whitetip and blacktip reef sharks and leopard sharks frequent these waters. Juveniles of the former can often be found resting beneath the table corals. Back at the main structure, in depths of around 5m (16ft), there is a selection of small creatures such as nudibranchs and wentletrap snails.

TOP *A longtail boat in the Had Nopparat National Park. These are often used as dive boats.*
RIGHT *A large, 2m-long (6.5ft) blotched fantail ray* (Taeniura meyeni) *skims the sea bed.*

KOH PHI PHI

The two islands of Koh Phi Phi Don and Koh Phi Phi Ley rise majestically from the ocean 47km (29 miles) southeast of Phuket. They form part of the Had Nopparat National Park, along with the two neighbouring islets of Koh Yung and Maisai. The smaller, more rugged island of Koh Phi Phi Ley is uninhabited, whereas its larger sister is now a bustling holiday retreat.

KOH PHI PHI DON

Located on the northwest coast of Koh Phi Phi Don is Ao Nui. The centre of this bay is marked by a prominent rocky outcrop, and the waters around this outcrop's eastern face are shallow and ideal for snorkelling. There are many corals and colourful reef fish among small boulders and rocks encrusted with patches of sponge. The opposite wall is heavily pitted with holes and tunnels of all sizes, which provide lairs for a variety of moray eels. Common lionfish, blue-ringed and emperor angelfish all flit around a narrow crevice that is littered with radiant corals and small sea fans.

Off the two southern prongs of Phi Phi Don, Hin Phae and Hin Dot are good snorkelling and diving destinations. Invertebrates abound, painted rock

lobster and a variety of small reef crabs mingling with busy cleaner and hingebeak shrimps as they tend to the dwellers of these domains. Laminates represent the majority of the hard corals.

The deeper sections of the walls have numerous oysters and clams clinging to, and embedded in, the craggy surface. Common reef octopuses secure themselves against the scattered rocks and lunge at any unsuspecting blennies that leave the security of their tiny burrows. Barracuda and other pelagics are also fairly common south of the reefs.

KOH BIDA NAI AND KOH BIDA NOK

South of the two Phi Phi islands lie two sheer rocky karsts, separated by a narrow 200m (656ft) channel. Named Koh Bida Nai (inner) and Koh Bida Nok (outer), both are great for observing small marine creatures, including squid and parrotfish.

ABOVE *A pair of amorous pharaoh cuttlefish* (Sepia pharaonis) *in a head-to-head mating ritual.*
BELOW *A coral head covered in soft corals.*

KOH LANTA

The Koh Lanta Marine National Park consists of 15 islands off the coast of Krabi Province. The region offers some of the best diving in the country, and the two jewels in the crown of this region are Hin Daeng and Hin Mouang. These sites are both around 50km (30 miles) and a five-hour boat ride southwest of the fishing port of Saladan, which serves the islands from its position on the northern extent of Koh Lanta Yai.

HIN DAENG AND HIN MOUANG

The quantity and health of both reef inhabitants and open ocean visitors is exceptional at both of these sites, which also attract enormous numbers of pelagics. These open ocean fish are often found in strong currents, and as the currents here tend to flow strongly, but not constantly, large schools come in to feed. Great, chevron and yellowtail barracuda, dogtooth tuna, rainbow runners, trevally, cobia and jacks are almost residential here.

Lastly, a much larger visitor provides more than welcome encounters – namely the enormous whale shark. This is one of the top destinations in the whole of Southeast Asia for encounters with this gentle giant. Another of the ocean's graceful creatures, the manta ray, is also a very frequent visitor to these dive sites.

LEFT *Chevron barracuda* (Sphyraena putnamiae) *are regularly seen at Hin Daeng and Hin Mouang.*
ABOVE *A majestic manta* (Manta breviostris).
BELOW *Close-up of the head of a Spanish dancer nudibranch* (Hexabranchus sanguinius).

HIN MOUANG

The best way to describe this rocky mass (which translates as Purple Rock), is as a series of inter-connected submerged pinnacles in varying depths descending from 8m (26ft). A garden of magnificent sea anemones carpets the top of the predominant pinnacle, their purple outer columns giving the site its name. The southernmost configuration begins as a sheer wall which descends to reach a narrow platform in about 40m (130ft) before it plummets down further, to in excess of 70m (230ft). There are a number of narrow valleys breaking the otherwise solid infrastructure, which are almost obscured by soft corals and gorgonian sea fans.

On closer inspection the latter feature longnose hawk-fish, soft coral crabs and – in the deeper waters – black coral shrimps, as familiar residents.

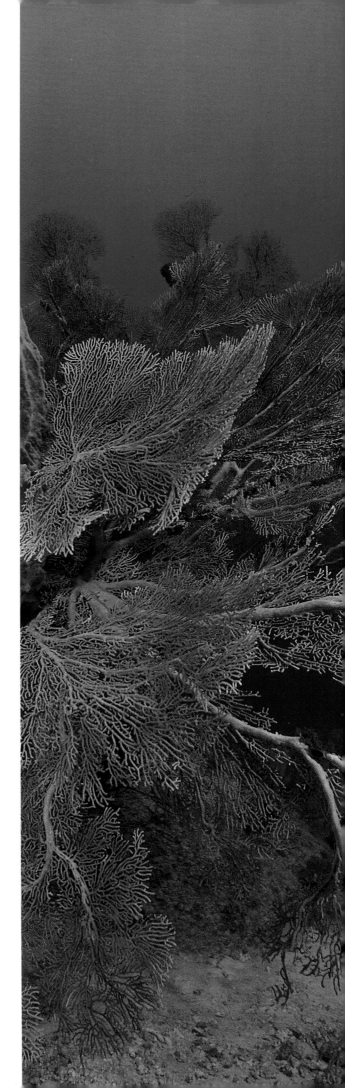

A prominent cavern approximately 50m (164ft) wide is found about midway along the length of the structure. It does not cut through the rock as do the smaller caverns, but instead breaks off halfway and changes course, splitting the structure rather than dividing it. In unkind currents this rocky blockade provides great shelter, and because of the diversity and colour of the marine life found in the gorge, it is not just a necessary shelter, but one of the highlights of the site! At night painted rock lobsters regimentally guard narrow shelves and tunnels in the walls, and the eyes of cleaner shrimps and minute reef crabs throw back the light in the form of tiny red dots. On a larger and more obvious scale, giant morays cause a temporary increase in divers' air consumption as they abandon their lairs for the night to participate, along with the motionless bearded scorpionfish, in their own particular style of nocturnal hunting.

ABOVE *The harlequin sweetlips* (Plectorhinchus chaetodonoides) *is a common reef resident.*
RIGHT *Situated at right angles to the water flow so as to filter out small prey, majestic gorgonian sea fans thrive in strong currents.*
FOLLOWING PAGES *A diver swims over giant plate corals.*

HIN DAENG

Unlike its close neighbour, Hin Daeng (which translates as Red Rock), does break the water's surface, but only at low tide. This rock's name comes courtesy of the hues of red *Dendro-nephthya* soft corals blanketing its upper slopes and walls. The rock continues its journey downwards as a series of walls and intermittent shelves and underwater plains in varying depths, these are all typically punctuated with varying amounts of coral boulders, sea whips and carpet anemones. The diversity of everyday reef life is grand at this rock and ranges from tiny inverte-brates to menacing-looking grey reef sharks that are ac-tually extremely timid and need not cause alarm – they are renowned for flee-ing upon the mere exhalation of a diver's bubbles.

Other sharks encountered at Hin Daeng include leopard sharks, and these are usually spotted around the southern section of the site. This area comprises two elevated ridges divided by a steep slope of small corals and more rocks, rather like a giant horseshoe.

The inner section is great for spotting a rather unusual selection of marine life, with no particu-lar pattern to it. Firstly there are cuttlefish and common reef octopus, after which are lionfish and scorpionfish and the odd stonefish, then morays, mantis shrimps and sea kraits. Schools of snappers are also present, but they tend to pass by. The leopard sharks seem content to chase after one another, cat-and-mouse style around and between small jutting pinnacles.

The centre section of this site reminds visitors of an oasis – but one that is surrounded by pinnacles rather than sand dunes. The effect is the same, however, as these pinnacles of rock provide shel-ter for the temporary inhabitants within. Stingrays, coral grouper and pufferfish are among the crea-tures to take advantage of this refuge.

Lastly, Hin Daeng has a large, resident green turtle, but knowing exactly where and when it will make an appearance remains impossible to predict. It just seems to appear from nowhere, and no one has ever tried to keep up with it in order to find out where it lives.

INDONESIA

Michael Aw

BALI • LOMBOK • ROTI • WEST TIMOR

The Indonesian islands of Sumatra, Java, Bali, Lombok, Sumba and Timor lie on the eastern rim of the Indian Ocean. This region is a crossroads of marine diversity, where species of the vast Pacific congregate with those of the Indian Ocean. Marine scientists recognise this region as the heartland of biodiversity – the richest and the most prolific in the world's marine flora and fauna.

Two of the world's foremost ichthyologists, Dr Gerry Allen and Dr Jack Randall, documented more than 3200 species of fish in Indonesian waters compared to just over 2000 in Palau, 1200 in Australia's Great Barrier Reef and about 800 in the Red Sea. The diversity of invertebrates such as corals, crustaceans, molluscs and worms is similarly wide. With such immense richness and equally varied terrain, like oceanic walls, canyons, submerged reefs and underwater volcanos, Indonesia is on the 'must visit' list of the discerning underwater adventurer. Comprised of more than 17,000 islands, Indonesia offers the intrepid a lifetime of exploration.

Although Indonesia is the world's largest Islamic country, Bali's population of 2.6 million is predominantly Hindu, celebrating a lifestyle of festivals, dance and music, based on philosophy, religion and organised principles. Of volcanic origin, the island's lush green vegetation, high mountains and white sand beaches make it one of Indonesia's most beautiful islands.

Bali is the international gateway to the rest of the archipelago, and tourism to the island yields over one million visitors per year. For this reason many divers snub Bali in favour of other less visited destinations. They are not aware that they are missing some very interesting dive sites. The *Liberty* wreck in Tulamben Bay is one of the most frequently dived World War II shipwrecks in the world. The renowned ichthyologist Robert Myers recorded nearly 600 species of fish here.

There are five main areas to dive in Bali: Nusa Dua and Sanur; Padang Bai and Candidasa; Nusa Penida and Lembongan; Tulamben and Menjangan. Each area is unique and offers suitable conditions for both beginners and seasoned divers.

East of Bali is the island of Lombok. Diving is done mainly around the three Gilis; Trawangan, Air and Meno, three sandy islands on the west coast of Lombok. They are idyllically tropical, with coconut palm foliage and extensive white sand beaches. Though surrounded by coral reefs and an impressive array of reef fish with a reasonable water visibility of around 15m (50ft), blast fishermen do operate in the area.

Diving off Roti and West Timor were initiated as side trips for divers venturing to Alor, a premier Eastern Indonesian destination. Although the diversity of marine species is similar to the rest of Indonesia, blast fishing is taking its toll.

Opposite Fishing boats at anchor in a small bay off a *gili*, or island.
Top right Lush plantations on Bali.

CLIMATE
Tropical monsoon climate.

BEST TIME TO GO
July and August

GETTING THERE
Flights to Jakarta and Denpasar in Bali.

WATER TEMPERATURE
BALI: Tulamben: 24–27°C (75–80.6°F); **Nusa Penida** and **Lembongan:** ocean upwellings cause dramatic variations. A drop from 24–15°C (75–59°F) is common; **Menjangan:** average 27°C (80.6°F); **Secret Bay:** average 21°C (69.8°F); **LOMBOK:** average 26°C (78.8°F); **ROTI:** 25–28°C (77–82°F); **WEST TIMOR:** 23 to 26°C (73 to 78.8°F)

VISIBILITY
BALI: Tulamben: average 20m (65ft), peak 25m (80ft); **Nusa Penida** and **Lembongan:** varies dramatically, from 5–30m (16–100ft); **Menjangan:** 20m (65ft); **Secret Bay:** about 10m (33ft) at high tide and 2–3m (6.5–10ft) at low tide. **LOMBOK:** average 15m (50ft); **ROTI:** varies from 5–15m (16–50ft); **WEST TIMOR:** averages 5–12m (16–40ft).

QUALITY OF MARINE LIFE
This region is the heartland of biodiversity. Tulamben Bay and Secret Bay, both on Bali, are particularly rich in species.

DEPTH OF DIVES
From 3m (10ft) to deeper than sport divers should dive.

SNORKELLING
On the *Liberty* wreck, Tulamben Bay, Bali.

BALI

TULAMBEN BAY

The coastal village of Tulamben is situated 120km (75 miles) northeast of Kuta, the main tourist belt of Bali. A small bay fringed by a pebbly beach is the point of entry to three of the best shore dives in Indonesia.

Unique to Tulamben is the porter service for scuba divers provided by women from the local village. From girls as young as 12 to grandmothers – all exhibit a prowess that will leave even the strongest divers agape. With a weight belt slung casually over their shoulder and wearing only rubber flip-flops, they carry the fully set up scuba tanks – complete with BCs and regulators – on their heads. Precariously balancing their loads of 20kg (44 lb) or more, they skillfully manoeuvre their way up and down the beach of fist-sized round pebbles with the posture of ballerinas. Even with rubber boots and nothing in hand, divers are often seen tripping over. The women are remunerated by the dive and resort operator, and the money is shared among the members of the village.

Amid the tranquillity it is hard to imagine that just 36 years ago, on March 17th 1963, Mount Agung exploded in a catastrophic eruption that swept away the entire village, killing more than 1000 people. Streams of lava and volcanic mud flowed through the area, completely smothering rice fields and roads, isolating this part of the island for quite a while. To this day the land remains barren and the rivers dry, but despite this the spirit of the village is one of gentleness, contentment and resilience. The landscape is astoundingly harsh – lontar palms and cactus spring up among lava rocks and dry river beds that meet the sea – its beauty sublime.

THE *LIBERTY* WRECK

Just 400m (1300ft) from Mimpi Resort lies the wreck of USAT *Liberty*, an impressive 100m-long (330ft) remnant of World War II. On January 11th 1942 a Japanese submarine torpedoed this armed vessel about 15km (9 miles) southwest of Lombok. While in tow by two destroyers, HMNS *Van Ghent* and USS *Paul Jones*, the *Liberty* began to take in water at a perilous rate. In an effort to salvage the cargo, she was successfully beached on the shores of Tulamben Bay. The violent eruption of 1963 toppled and pushed the vessel back into the water, to come to rest almost parallel to shore. Today, she is Indonesia's diving mascot.

However, it is neither the structure nor history that attracts divers from all over the world, but the density and quality of marine life found on her. The vessel is a showpiece of the richness of Indonesia's marine biodiversity. The ease with which you can dive the wreck, which extends from a depth of 5 down to 30m (16 to 100ft), also has a lot to do with its popularity.

The most obvious attraction on the wreck is the number and variety of friendly fish. Sergeant-major damselfish, unicornfish and crescent wrasse often swim right up to divers, to request a free feed. The bigger fish, including bumphead parrotfish, Napoleon wrasse, Oriental sweetlips, rabbitfish, coral and other groupers, sometimes

---

hover in midwater, making excellent photographic subjects for fish portraits.

More than 600 species of reef fish are found in and around the wreck. Although only a few table-sized hard corals are found on its outer edge, the superstructure is heavily colonized by soft corals, gorgonian sea fans, and tall black coral trees, stinging hydrozoan and colourful sponges.

The gun is still intact on the stern at 28m (90ft), completely encrusted with sessile animals and sea fans. At 30m (100ft), the wreck is prolific with red sea whips, huge barrel sponges and numerous species of gobies – it is a marine photographer's dream location. Even snorkellers can enjoy themselves on the wreck; the bow, heavily encrusted with sponges, sea squirts and a haven for friendly fish, is a mere 30m (100ft) swim from shore.

THE WALL

On the eastern end of the bay, beneath the temple, is a coral wall that plummets to beyond 60m (200ft). This is where the fantasies of many divers dwell. The wall is completely covered with huge barrel sponges, coral trees and oversized gorgonian sea fans. One gorgonian sea fan, prominently positioned on a ledge at 30m (100ft), is more than 3m (10ft) high and is adorned with longnose hawkfish and golden damselfish. Hiding in numerous caverns and crevices there are thorny oysters, *Tubastrea* corals, crabs, and shrimps sharing homes with squirrelfish, coral groupers, blennies and scorpionfish.

Among fish experts, this wall is famous for harbouring hard-to-find species including the comet (*Calloplesiops altivelis*), a fish with elaborate fins

and a false eyespot. Night-time on The Wall is like an undersea presentation of Walt Disney's *Fantasia*, played continuously through the night. To enjoy the show, face the wall, switch off your torch and watch. Millions of tiny green bulbs will appear, as if by magic, to perform a show of twinkling, zigzagging lights.

MIMPI HOUSE REEF

Leading authors of marine books including Rudie Kuiter, Roger Steen and Gerry Allen shared a secret – the best place to hunt for new species in the bay is not on the wreck, nor on the wall. The best place to search for rare, unusual creatures is in among the congregations of crinoids, sponges and anemones scattered across the vast black sand slopes just off Mimpi. Probing will reveal numerous harlequin ghost pipefish, sea horses, 15 species of nudibranchs, devilfish, helmet gurnards, shrimp gobies, rare squat lobsters, squid, snake eels, sea spiders, anemone crabs and yet-to-be described species of sand anemone.

The best way to dive Tulamben is to stay at Mimpi Resort or Paradise Home, located right on

the beachfront. Staying right on site gives you the freedom of unlimited diving and the option of early morning or evening dives to avoid the hundreds of day-tripper divers that show up after 10:00 from Kuta. Between 10:00 and 15:00, there is heavy traffic on the *Liberty* wreck.

The other option is to join one of the dive operators for a day trip, which starts from Kuta at 07:00. Despite the long car journey, the trip is worthwhile for a taste of the diving at Tulamben. Serious divers claim that 10 days is barely enough to explore the many delights of this bay.

NUSA PENIDA AND LEMBONGAN

The islands of Penida, Lembongan and Cenida lie in a tightly packed group just off the southeast coast of Bali. The Bandung Strait not only separates these islands from mainland Bali, but it is also part of the Wallace Line, an imaginary border that separates the flora and fauna of the East from that of the West. The natural environment here is distinctly different from that of Bali and Java.

Although Bali is a mere 11km (7 miles) away, this is an entirely different world in every sense. In this region huge volumes of water are incessantly flushed between the Indian Ocean and the Java Sea. Deep, icy ocean upwelling, downwelling and fast currents furnish the reef systems with rich nutrients. Diving here can be treacherous for the inexperienced, but certainly provides a rush of adrenaline for the well prepared.

BELOW *A diver moves through a seascape near the wreck of the* Liberty *at Tulamben Bay in Bali. The wreck is a focal point for a profusion of marine life including more than 600 species of reef fish.*

JURASSIC POINT

As one dive operator described diving Jurassic Point, near Lembongan Island: 'this is one of those places that can be the best, worst or last dive you will ever have'! The standard profile is a reef terrace at 10m (30ft), then a precipitous drop to 30m (100ft), followed by a gentle slope to 600m

oceanic, living on a diet of jellyfish and plankton. Molas are surreal, big and deceptively slow, they tantalize closer investigation – but one wrong move by a diver will cause these seemingly soporific fish to vanish in a flash. Swimming with an ocean sunfish is an experience to die for; once, twice, thrice and never enough.

the diving here is safe and easy, making it a major haunt for divers of all levels. However, the reefs and walls are wonderful, prolific, and provide an excellent sample of the terrain and marine fauna of underwater Indonesia.

Menjangan Island is rugged, with caves, grottos and crevices, and only a couple of small sandy

(1970ft). Pinnacles and rocky outcrops are found along the 30m (100ft) level. Once off the reef terrace, the structure is similar to the odd terrain on the surface – but covered with a meadow of multi-coloured soft stumpy corals. The abundance of reef life supports many big groupers, sharks and tuna. Eagle rays and hundreds of giant reef rays sometimes congregate to mate among the ledges and crevices. Because of the narrow channel, pelagics cruise close to the wall, well within range of the passing divers. Once you are in the swift current, you will no longer just be watching the pelagics – you will literally become one of them.

Perhaps the single most attractive lure to diving Jurassic Point are the ocean sunfish, *Mola mola*, that make frequent appearances here between the months of August and November. Growing up to 3m (10ft) across, these oddballs of the sea are shaped like a flying saucer with two wings in the 'wrong' places. Two huge fins, one on the top and one on the bottom, a disc-shaped gelatinous body, big bulbous eyes and a tiny mouth make them look totally uncoordinated, like a creature evolved from a bad joke. Ocean sunfish belong to the family Molidae, and as their name suggests, are totally

MANTA POINT

Another, equally good site is Manta Point, on the west coast of Penida. Swift currents bring huge school of jacks, and the experience of swimming with large groups of mantas in shallow water. Being nudged by more than 20 of these gentle giants is not uncommon here. Although there are predictable manta encounters in other places, the Penida manta experience is almost spiritual; seeing them vanishing and materializing in and out of milky blue water is like watching a ballet in a sky of endless puffy clouds.

Most decent dive operators in Bali offer day trips to the Penida group of islands. Boats usually depart from Sanur, but the bigger day-boats depart from Benoa Harbour, and prior arrangement is necessary. Your best bet to see the ocean sunfish is with Michael Cortenbach of Bali Hai Cruises. He has conducted behavioural research on this fish for a number of years.

MENJANGAN

Menjangan Island is located just offshore of the northwestern corner of Bali. Part of the Bali Barat National Park, it is a protected reserve, and thus access is restricted to daylight hours. Because the island is sheltered from strong currents and surge,

ABOVE (left to right) *A brittle star* (Ophiothela *sp.*); *a jewel-box sea urchin* (Mespilia globulus); *a jellyfish* (Phyllorhiza punctata) – *favoured diet of sunfish.*
LEFT *A big fin reef squid* (Sepioteuthis lessoniana).

beaches. The reef top is prolific with *Acropora* corals, but aesthetically scarred by anchor and diver damage. The coral walls and slopes are lush with huge barrel sponges, red sea whips and gorgonian sea fans. Batfish, surgeonfish and parrotfish dominate the fish fauna, and whitetip reef sharks are found in deeper water. Though the coral walls extend deeper than 60m (200ft), life forms are most abundant on the reef slope and wall from 10 to 30m (33 to 100ft).

The best dive site is just south of the eastern end of the island. To find it, descend to about 18m (60ft) and follow the terrain in a northeasterly direction among fields of gorgonian and whip corals. Another site of interest is the *Anker* wreck. It is located at 30m (100ft) depth, on the western tip of the island. The stern of the 25m-vessel (80ft) rests on the sandy bottom at 45m (150ft), and is encrusted with corals and gorgonians. The fish life is usually dense, comprising snappers, Moorish idols, sweetlips and parrotfish.

To dive Menjangan it is necessary to join one of the local operators based in Kuta or Sanur. The

OCEAN SUNFISH

The ocean sunfish (Mola mola) is one of the most enigmatic creatures in the ocean. Endowed with a disc-shaped body, a huge pectoral and anal fin, swollen lips on a tiny mouth on one end and an ineffectual tail on the other, sunfish are naturally fascinating.

Found near or at the surface in all tropical and temperate waters, sunfish are flat, round, open-ocean oddballs related to reef pufferfish. Perhaps it is their round shape and their habit of turning on their side on the surface of the sea that inspired the name sunfish, but in some areas they are referred to as moonfish.

The ocean sunfish is the world's largest bony fish; the biggest on record is 3.3m (11ft) head-to-tail, weighing 2235kg (4928 lb). Among other distinguishing features, these fish have an extremely thick mucous-coated rubbery skin. On an adult, the skin is more than 12cm (5in) thick.

Sunfish have most effective natural defences; they are full of parasites and not nice to eat, and supposedly they are huge in numbers (mind you, they are not easy to find). Sunfish are also known to be the most fecund of all fish in the ocean; a metre-plus female may shed more than 300 million eggs.

Because they dwell mostly near ocean surfaces, the ocean sunfish's diet consists mostly of floating animals. Jellyfish are their favourite food. The sunfish literally suck in their prey, hold the food in their long claw-like throat teeth, then spit the water out.

While sunfish are mostly seen on the surface, sometimes with birds pecking the parasites off their bodies, in Bali they are usually seen in blue water or at 30m (100ft), with an accompanying host of bannerfish, angelfish and wrasses.

RIGHT A scuba diver is dwarfed by an ocean sunfish (Mola mola), accompanied by a school of attendant longfin bannerfish (Heniochus acuminatus).

125km (78 mile) car ride from the tourist belt is scenic and the dive package usually includes two tank dives, return boat and car transfer from a city hotel, weight belts, lunch and park fees.

SECRET BAY

This new site is proprietary to Tonozuka, the best-known fish photographer in Bali. Since its discovery, Secret Bay is on the wish list of every serious underwater photographer in Asia and Japan. Many species new to science are currently being recorded in this bay.

Located just across the road from Gilimanuk, the ferry crossing point to Java, the entry point to the bay is occupied by a new dive centre specially developed to service the influx of underwater photographers. Secret Bay is an easy shore dive, but the water is usually cold as a result of the nearby deep-water cold currents, which are directed into the bay by regular upwellings and tides. Nutrient-rich colder water blends with this sea grass and mangrove environment, making this a special nursery for both Pacific and Indian Ocean animals. Many species found here are endemic to the site, and others are rare in other parts of Bali or even the rest of Indonesia.

The site is unique in Bali, as it is mostly shallow with a maximum depth of 3m (10ft). The black sandy bottom of the bay is covered with loose seaweed and sargassum. Once beneath the surface the trained observer will find creature heaven; sea horses, spotfin lionfish, harlequin ghost pipefish, snake eels, stonefish, nudibranchs, gobies, dragonets, sea urchins, exotic species of cardinalfish and frogfish. Frogfish in particular are abundant and diverse in the bay; four different species are found here including the spotfin, sargassum, the picta and a species currently awaiting scientific description.

At low tide, the visibility and density of rare creatures will cause macrophotographers to redefine the meaning of 'muck diving' (searching out small creatures in the shallows). Secret Bay is not for the ordinary diver, but if new discoveries, macrophotography and exotic marine life stimulate you, then this is the site for you.

Currently the only way to dive Secret Bay is by arrangement with Tonozuka at Dive & Dive Bali. To prevent exploitation of the location, the operator is determined to protect the site from mass tourism – hence the name Secret Bay.

TOP LEFT *A fingered dragonet* (Dactylopus dactylopus). BELOW (left to right) *Painted frogfish* (Antennarius pictus); *a sea horse* (Hippocampus *sp.*); *a snake eel* (Ophichthidae *sp.*) *peers out of the substrate.*

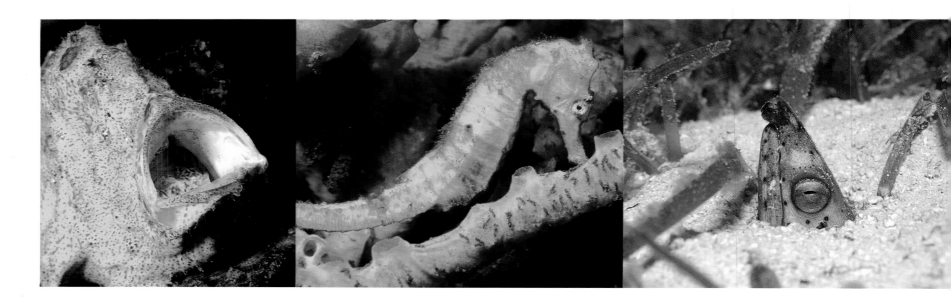

LOMBOK

TAKAT MALANG

This site is located north of Gili Air, the island closest to Lombok, and is by far the best dive site in the area. The hard coral meadows here are impressive; Dr Carden Wallace of the Museum of Tropical Queensland found the site to be one of the most diverse in *Acropora* species in the Indo-Pacific. During the survey, a number of new species were discovered and named.

Large schools of jacks or trevally are consistently sighted here, including a few giant specimens of *Caranx ignobilis*. Whitetip reef sharks are also regularly sighted here – as many as 10 are sometimes found in the deeper channel. This is a relatively easy dive that guarantees to entertain both beginners and experienced divers.

TRAWANGAN SOFT CORAL GARDEN

Aptly named, this site is along the north coast of Gili Trawangan and is covered with gorgonian sea fans, *Dendronephytha* soft corals, sponges and lacy corals. Most often a current of one to two knots is running, and thus a drift dive is necessary along the steep slope. Large dogtooth tuna sometime venture close in to check out divers, and large numbers of bluestriped snappers, emperor angelfish, lyretail and yellowstriped anthias are prolific among the coral outcrops.

On the eastern end of the coral garden are a few coral outcrops with healthy corals and reef fish. Blue-spotted stingrays, moray eels and sand gobies are some of the obvious inhabitants. Notably, a couple of giant clams in the vicinity are some of the biggest remaining in Indonesian waters.

Five dive operators, some with dive bases on Gili Trawangan, support divers visiting Lombok. They vary in operational standard, but the larger ones offer training up to instructor level and surprisingly a couple of them offer Nitrox and mixed gas diving. As July and August are the peak season, it is essential to make arrangements in advance.

OPPOSITE TOP RIGHT *An overview of Lombok showing Api Banda Volcano.*

RIGHT *A diver explores Trawangan Soft Coral Garden.*

ROTI

Lying off the southwestern tip of West Timor is the island of Roti, which is also Indonesia's southernmost point in the Indian Ocean. Although to date the diving here has been mostly exploratory, the two most outstanding sites charted are Batu Termanu Mai, the female rock, and Batu Termanu Jantan, the male rock.

BATU TERMANU MAI

Batu Termanu Mai, the bigger of the two rocks, is located northeast of Ba'a the island capital. Sheer rugged limestone formations plunge steeply into the water here. The reef flat is extensive, spreading more than 100m (330ft) before dropping down a wall to 30m (100ft). The soft coral coverage on this wall is the equivalent of the White Wall of Fiji; pastel coloured soft corals and orange *Tubastrea* corals carpet the entire wall.

In deeper water, the green *Tubastrea* and black coral trees take over as the dominant coverage. Yellowback fusiliers, surgeonfish, butterflyfish and wrasse swim up and down the wall, while eagle rays and mackerel parade in the blue water. Whitetip reef sharks and large groupers often hang out in a number of small caverns, and

under ledges. Longnose hawkfish and some large lionfish are also often encountered here.

BATU TERMANU JANTAN

Batu Termanu Jantan, the smaller of the two rocks, is a 15-minute boat-ride east of Batu Termanu Mai. It is a roundish rock with a satellite pinnacle, and at high tide only the pinnacle is visible. On its seaward side there are numerous narrow swim-throughs or passages between coral outcrops that are excellent for exploration. Lobsters, whitetip reef sharks and groupers are found resting on ledges and in crevices.

Although mantas are often sighted, swirling jacks and barracuda are almost always found around the rock. During our exploratory expedition, we were hugely surprised to find a 6m-long (20ft) juvenile whale shark at 12m (40ft) depth, swimming alongside us to feed on a black cloud of bait fish. Though visibility was only about 8m (26ft), swimming with this gentle giant for more than 15 minutes was one of those ecstatic episodes of underwater exploration.

No known diving facilities operate on Roti. The best way to dive it is with a live-aboard expedition from Maumere, the dive capital of East Flores.

Map labels:
SAVU SEA
WEST TIMOR
Batu Termanu Mai and Batu Termanu Jantan
Ndao
ROTI
BA'A
ARAFURA SEA
Dana

ABOVE *A trumpetfish* (Aulostomis chinensis).
BELOW LEFT *An unusual photograph showing an olive sea snake* (Aepisurus laevis) *devouring an eel.*
BELOW *Royal blue tunicate* (Rhopalaea *sp.*).

WENTLETRAP SNAILS (EPITONIUM BILEEANUM)

In the scheme of bedtime stories and fairy tales, wolves are victims of the necessities of life — they need to eat to live and are damned for it. The 'wolf in sheep's clothing' is being ingenious, but by doing so is condemned for its natural instincts and craftiness. In the marine kingdom, there is a particular trickster with plenty of attitude and

females generally feast on separate coral animals, but may occasionally dine on a single victim.

It is unclear to marine biologists whether the snails are immune to the stinging cells of their prey. However, it seems that, with the aid of a powerful rubbery proboscis, Epitonium bileeanum is able to keep a safe distance from any stinging tentacles.

IMPACT ON CORALS

Epitonium bileeanum is known to have a hefty appetite. After an invasion by a flock of these wentletrap snails, few coral polyps will have escaped the massacre. An entire colony of Tubastrea may be wiped out during the course of an afternoon.

intelligence, Epitonium bileeanum, a species of marine snail belonging to the group of wentletraps, that has emulated the 'wolf in sheep's clothing' stratagem.

These wolves of the sea don a cheerful canary-yellow suit and assume a seemingly innocent appearance, whereas they are in fact notorious for literally sucking the life out of their still-living prey, and thereafter using their victim's cadaver as a nest for their offspring.

FEEDING HABITS

Discerning in their culinary pursuits, these wentletraps feed exclusively on Tubastrea, a hard, brightly orange-and-yellow-coloured tube coral found on the reefs of the Indo-Pacific Ocean. In the society of wentletraps the male is smaller, and hitches a ride on the back of his partner en route to perform the two essential chores in evolution — to eat and to procreate.

Epitonium bileeanum prey on the sunflower-coloured Tubastrea coccinea, which is widely distributed through-out the tropics. Since Tubastrea are not dependent on sunlight, they are mostly found under overhangs, in caves and along steep walls. Their tentacles are equipped with stinging cells used to trap plankton in passing currents.

Once they have located their prey, these wentletrap snails proceed to devour it by sucking out its tissue. Males and

REPRODUCTION

Few of us are capable of eating while procreating, but female Epitonium bileeanum have no problem perform-ing this feat. Even while depositing eggs on a deceased victim, they continue to feed on another victim. The yellow egg-mass is deposited in strings of tiny yellow whorls and loops that resemble extended Tubastrea tentacles at close range. By mimicking the stinging tentacles of the Tubastrea coral, the brood is well protected from other predators.

ABOVE LEFT A wentletrap snail with its long, rubbery proboscis extended into a live coral cup.

ABOVE CENTRE Wentletraps can mate and feed at the same time. The males are smaller than the females.

ABOVE The shape and coloration of the eggs resemble the tentacles of Tubastrea coral.

BELOW This wentletrap snail is feeding on a living coral polyp, amid the gutted remains of those it has already devoured.

WEST TIMOR

KUPANG

While it is possible to dive Kupang all year round, the known dive sites are mostly around the harbour area, the northeast of Semau Island and the nearby island of Kera. Of particular interest to underwater photographers is the coral slope off the Pertamina Dock. This is undoubtedly a fantastic dive site for enthusiasts of macrophotography as well as those who are intrigued by strange creatures. There are pipefish, frogfish, scorpionfish, ribbon eels, decorated crabs, colourful nudibranchs, and harlequin ghost pipefish in abundance, mostly on the reef top and edge. For, although the reef falls to about 15m (50ft), most creatures inhabit the shallower depths. This site is excellent for night dives, where squid, lionfish, shrimps, snails and crabs reveal themselves to play out the cycles of life. Moray eels and octopus are often seen leaving their holes to feed. The great diversity of invertebrates on this dive site provides the underwater photographer with endless opportunities.

SEMAU ISLAND

Semau Island is located just off the coast of West Timor, and there are a couple of good dive sites off the island's northeast coast. Just southeast of the northern tip of the island is a coral wall with numerous caverns, some with 6m-deep (20ft) chambers. Although the visibility is never great here, the caverns make for interesting exploration. The reef top is close to shore, varying from 2 to 5m (6.5 to 16ft) in depth, and plunges quickly down 20 to 40m (65 to 130ft). Whereas white soft corals, gorgonian sea fans and purple sponges adorn the shallower depths, black coral trees are found at greater depths.

Several species of groupers, sweetlips, snappers, squirrelfish and stingrays move back and forth continuously between the caverns. The intensive fishing activities are obvious; the fish are skittish and shy away from divers. However, at the time of our exploratory expedition, we sighted six bumphead parrotfish grazing on the reef top and a lone adult Napoleon wrasse sleeping in a cavern at 25m (80ft).

South of the cavern walls, the reef structure tapers off to a point at Tanjung Kataba. The hard coral meadow here is excellent, comprising of diverse species of *Montipora*, *Acropora* and *Galaxea* corals. Redtooth triggerfish swamp the reef slope by the thousand. In deeper water, large thresher sharks may be seen hanging out at the edge of visibility.

There is one known full-time operator on the island, but the best way to go is with a live-aboard boat from Maumere, a popular Indonesian dive destination on Flores, northwest of Timor.

BELOW LEFT *Longnose hawkfish* (Oxycirrhites typus).
BELOW *Mantis shrimp* (Odontodactylus scyllarus).
OPPOSITE *A current-swept sea fan with anthias, wrasse and feather stars on sponges. Large volumes of water flow from the Indian Ocean into Indonesia, bringing rich nutrients to support a lush diversity of reef life.*

Map labels: SAVU SEA, Kera Island, Tulong, Semau Island, WEST TIMOR, KUPANG, ARAFURA SEA, ROTI

AUSTRALIA

Ann Storrie and Rebecca Saunders

COCOS ISLANDS · CHRISTMAS ISLAND · SCOTT REEF TO HMAS *SWAN* · NEPTUNE ISLANDS

Nearly one third of Australia's 20,000km (12,430-mile) coastline occurs in the state of Western Australia, and most of this coast is washed by the Indian Ocean. It ranges from the tropical coral reefs off the Kimberly coast to the temperate granite and limestone habitats of the southwest. Offshore to the northwest lies Christmas Island, and further still, the Cocos Islands. When the Western Australian continental shelf subsided about 10 million years ago, it left a band of perfectly formed oceanic atolls that extend for hundreds of kilometres along the northwestern coastline. These atolls, which include Rowley Shoals, Scott and Seringapatam reefs, provide some of the most pristine and exciting tropical reef diving in the world. It has only been within the last 10 to 15 years that this area started to be explored, and there is still much to be discovered.

Further south, tropical and temperate waters mix. At Exmouth and Coral Bay, a wonderful range of marine life shares interesting habitats along the Ningaloo Reef, which is the longest fringing reef in the world. Whale sharks congregate here each year to feed on plankton after the coral spawn, and the reef and its environs is home to thousands of reef fish, turtles, dugong, and invertebrates.

This area boasts the picturesque scenery of the Cape Range National Park as well as beautiful,

safe bays for snorkellers. The deeper dives on the outer reef allow encounters with sharks, mantas and other large fish that astound even seasoned divers.

The southwest of Western Australia has delightful temperate marine environments. Limestone and granite pinnacles, caves, ledges and overhangs brim with invertebrates, the colour of which rivals that of tropical coral reefs. There are Marine Parks right on Perth's (the capital city's) doorstep, which serve both to protect marine life and allow people to indulge in many of their favourite activities such as fishing and collecting crays (western rock lobsters). Some of the best dive sites occur just a stone's throw from Perth's main swimming beaches, and off Rottnest Island, which lies 11km (7 miles) off the coast. Wrecks are also a feature along the Western Australian coastline. There are 17th-century vessels to be discovered, and the recently scuttled Australian warship HMAS *Swan* is now a major dive attraction in the southwest.

With increasing tourism, the dive industry in Australia has become extremely efficient. Diving can be arranged on arrival for most areas along the coast. However, some remote areas, such as Rowley Shoals and Scott Reef, require prior preparation and planning.

Those seeking an adrenaline-rush need look no further than cage dives with great white sharks off the Neptune Islands, South Australia.

Opposite An overview of a section of Ningaloo Reef, showing Point Billie on the Exmouth Peninsula.
Above right Boats moored in Geordie Bay on Rottnest Island, with Fays Bay in the foreground.

CLIMATE

The north is tropical, the far south temperate. Northern summer land temperatures vary from 26–30°C (79–86°F) as far south as Ningaloo Reef, reaching 38°C (100°F) at Coral Bay. Neptune Islands average 20°C (68°F).

BEST TIME TO GO

Cocos and **Christmas islands:** all year. **Scott Reef, Seringapatam, Rowley Shoals:** August/September. **Ningaloo Reef:** April–November. **Coral Bay:** April–October. **Rottnest Island:** October–June. **HMAS *Swan*:** February–May. **Neptune Islands:** January–April.

GETTING THERE

Cocos and **Christmas islands:** International flights to Perth and Jakarta, connecting flights to the islands. **Western Australia:** flights to Perth. **Neptune Islands:** flights to Adelaide.

WATER TEMPERATURE

Cocos, Christmas Islands, Scott Reef, Seringapatam: average 28°C (82°F). **Rowley Shoals, Ningaloo, Coral Bay:** 25°C (77°F). **Rottnest Island, HMAS *Swan*:** 20°C (68°F). **Neptune Islands:** 16°C (60.8°F).

VISIBILITY

Average better than 20m (65ft).

QUALITY OF MARINE LIFE

Good, with some pristine coral reefs. Divers come to see whale sharks and great whites.

DEPTH OF DIVES

Deep at Christmas Island and Seringapatam.

SNORKELLING

Cocos, Rowley Shoals, Ningaloo, Coral Bay.

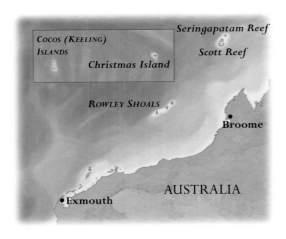

COCOS ISLANDS

The Cocos (Keeling) Islands lie approximately 2760km (1715 miles) northwest of Perth, and 1000km (620 miles) southwest of Java (at about 12°30′S and 96°30′E). They consist of two atolls that have been Australian territories since 1955. The southern atoll (Cocos Island) has 25 small sand cays which surround a 15km-long (9-mile) lagoon. Another large island, North Keeling, lies approximately 24km (15 miles) to the north. The latter is uninhabited and is an important bird and wildlife sanctuary.

These islands are true coral atolls. During Charles Darwin's visit in 1836 the southern atoll provided him with evidence to formulate his theories on coral atoll formation. He hypothesized that the growth of corals continued long after the seamounts that supported them had subsided. Below Cocos Island's thin veneer of beautiful living coral lies between 500 and 1000m (1640 and 3280ft) of cemented limestone.

Cocos is renowned for its large pelagic fish, reef sharks, manta rays, giant humphead (Napoleon) wrasse (known locally as Maori wrasse), turtles, and the many varied coral growths around the atoll. Dive sites offer such diversity that it is hard to believe that they are only a kilometre or two apart. The Tablelands lie on the northeast corner of Direction Island, where enormous *Acropora* plate corals stack up from 25m (82ft) to the surface. The Cabbage Patch is only a few kilometres to the west, yet there is not a 'table' in sight. Here, thousands of *Turbinaria* corals lie side by side, forming an enormous 'vegetable garden' that is covered in colourful basslets and queenfish. At The Garden of Eden, brilliant orange and red gorgonians adorn a small drop-off, and thousands of reef fish dart among a variety of hard corals growing on top of the wall.

A few very easy dives or snorkels can also be done around the Cocos group. The Coal Barge

---

ABOVE *Prison Island in the Cocos group.*
BELOW (left to right) *A vivid Bullock's nudibranch* (Hypselodoris bullocki); *a large blue crab* (Cardisoma carnifex); *a seascape near Horsburgh Island.*

near Horsburgh Island is only about 2m (6.5ft) deep and the water is usually very clear and calm. The barge is covered in invertebrates with many *Pocillopora* and *Acropora* corals growing on the superstructure. Powder-blue surgeonfish and angelfish are permanent residents, and large

---

ABOVE *The Rip, near Direction Island.*
BELOW (left to right) *A spotted garden eel* (Heteroconger hassi)*; a snorkeller encounters a whitetip reef shark* (Triaenodon obesus)*.

schools of sea perch are always found around the wreck. The Rip is a channel between Direction and Home Island, which provides a fast drift-dive. Here, hundreds of reef fish hide under ledges and resident whitetip reef sharks are nearly always seen lying on the sand.

Diving on the Cocos Islands is generally very relaxing and easy. The climate is tropical and land temperatures vary between 23 and 29°C (73 and 84°F) year round. The average water temperature is 27°C (80°F) and average visibility is 20m (65ft), although it can be as good as 30 to 50m (100 to

164ft) from December to February. The wettest months are April to June, and the driest September to November. December to April is the cyclone season, but few sweep directly over Cocos. The islands can thus be dived all year round. If a cyclone passes close during the summer months, a couple of days may be lost.

Diving facilities are excellent, and there are a number of sights to see between dives, including beautiful coconut-palm-lined beaches, local wildlife and World War II guns. There are flights to Cocos Island from Perth and Christmas Island.

CHRISTMAS ISLAND

Christmas Island is one of the remotest and least known of Australia's island territories. It is a small volcanic atoll, 2600km (1615 miles) northwest of Perth and 360km (223 miles) south of Jakarta (10°30'S and 105°40'E). For much of the last century, its rainforests were mined for phosphate. More recently, however, the scientific importance of the island's unique ecosystems has taken precedence and phosphate mining is now carried out only on previous stockpiles. Sixty-three per cent of both the island's 135km² (52 sq. miles) of land and 73km (45 miles) of coastline is national park.

Christmas Island is especially renowned for its magnificent bird life, the annual crab migration (when over 130 million red crabs make their way from the tropical rain forest to spawn in the ocean), and its sheer wall diving. The island's topography is spectacular, both above and below the sea. Its volcanic origins, and uplifts which occurred many millions of years ago, left jagged island terraces, a central plateau and sheer limestone cliffs that plummet 10 to 20m (30 to 65ft) into the surrounding ocean. The cliffs are interspersed with occasional small sand and shingle beaches. A narrow reef extends offshore and rock pools form on sea-level terraces. The drop-offs feature many undercuts, caves and fissures.

Christmas Island is an ancient volcano that rises 4300m (14,100ft) from the sea bed, and there are very few dives around the island that are not wall dives. Even at the island's settlement at Flying Fish Cove – where a small beach, jetty and gantry service the phosphate shipping and boating community – the diving is spectacular. Less than 100m

offshore the wall drops into 200 fathoms (360m; 1200ft) of water. There are also areas of sloping walls here for less adventurous divers.

As with any isolated atoll, many marine species have proliferated while others have not yet colonized the area. Of the fish, the absence of coral groupers, humbug damsels and dragonets is countered by the abundance of other groupers, wrasse, damselfish, gobies, butterflyfish, surgeonfish, blennies and cardinalfish. Many of these species thrive in above-average numbers compared with other Indo-Pacific localities.

Scorpionfish and stonefish have found their niche in the shallow waters of Flying Fish Cove. A favourite area for enormous stonefish is around the Cantilevers, or the gantry where the phosphate

ships are loaded. Several colourful species of scorpionfish congregate around the jetty and boat ramp beside the island's best swimming beach. Eels are also very common here. There are giant morays, white-mouthed morays, spotted morays, blue-ribbon eels, garden eels and even magnificent dragon morays. Three or four of these species may be seen on every dive.

The corals are spectacular with enormous gorgonians and colourful soft corals growing on the

ABOVE *Flying Fish Cove at dusk.*
BELOW (left to right) *Dragon moray eel* (Enchelycore pardalis); *a helmet gurnard* (Dactyloptena sp.); *and a red crab* (Gecarcoidea natalis).

vertical walls. Black coral is also abundant on some of the steep drop-offs around the island.

Accessibility to various dive sites is dependent on the weather. The climate is tropical. During the summer months, the northwesterly winds may inhibit diving from Flying Fish Cove, but diving on the east coast can usually be arranged at this time. The water temperature averages 28°C (82°F) and visibility on the walls is generally between 30 and 50m (100 and 164ft). During summer, in the cyclone season, visibility may be less and a day or two's diving may be lost if a cyclone passes close to the island.

There are regular flights from Perth and Jakarta to Christmas Island, and for nine months of the year Flying Fish Cove is the perfect base. Otherwise, a site on the opposite side of the island can be used. If you have time, it is well worth visiting the rainforests. Red crabs, blue swimming crabs and the giant robber crabs can always be seen. Other areas of interest on Christmas Island include the Blowholes, Greta Beach, Hugh's Waterfall and The Dales.

ABOVE *The elaborately camouflaged spiny devilfish* (Inimicus didactylus) *is very poisonous.*
RIGHT *Reefscape showing the biodiversity of corals in an area that experiences strong current action.*

SCOTT REEF AND SERINGAPATAM ATOLL

Scott Reef and Seringapatam Atoll lie approximately 400km (250 miles) northwest of Broome in Western Australia (around 121°46'E and 14°S). They are extremely isolated atolls, and one small sand cay, about 200m (656ft) long and barren of vegetation, is the only permanent dry land. Even their reefs are submerged at high tide. Scott Reef consists of the crescent-shaped South Reef, and a huge, pear-shaped reef called North Reef. The coral rim of North Reef is breached in two places, and allows boat access to a 15km-wide (9-mile) lagoon. The sand cay, Sandy Islet, lies just to the northeast of West Hook, which is the westerly tip of South Reef. Seringapatam is a tiny atoll approximately 50km (30 miles) northeast of Scott Reef.

These reefs offer some of the most pristine, varied and exciting diving in tropical Australia. There are sheer walls on the southern side of South Reef and northern Seringapatam. Huge gorgonian sea fans, soft *Alcyonarian* corals, long fronds of black coral, brilliant red sea whips, large sponges, hard coral overhangs and thousands of encrusting invertebrates adorn these walls. Small reef fish abound, while large schools of bumphead parrotfish, Napoleon wrasse, surgeonfish, reef sharks and manta rays are also quite common here.

Another plentiful creature on these reefs is the sea snake. Surprisingly, they have never been reported at the Rowley Shoals, 400km (250 miles) southwest of Scott Reef, yet Scott Reef, Seringapatam and Ashmore Reef (further north), have the largest sea snake population in the world.

You may find as many as 20 snakes on each dive. Beautiful, inquisitive and sometimes extremely friendly snakes of several species may follow divers during most of their time underwater. Provided the snakes are not antagonized, they are rarely a problem. It is a wonderful experience to gently glide through the calm waters of North Reef

lagoon and watch the sea snakes gently winding their way through the branches of staghorn corals and poking into crevices for prey.

Drift diving into and out of North Reef lagoon is a thrilling experience. Depending on the time of day, you can pick your drift from a leisurely glide through the channel to a ripping roller coaster ride, dodging enormous coral heads and the edges of the reef as you swirl into or out of the lagoon. For the shark enthusiasts, a drift from inside the lagoon sometimes culminates in your being deposited in front of a large line of reef sharks that wait for the smorgasbord to emerge from the channel. But be careful – you are part of the smorgasbord.

Diving these remote atolls is not for the faint-hearted or novice diver. There are no facilities, save for the chartered live-aboard, and you are a couple of days away from the mainland's nearest town. Diving can be deep. The wall on Seringa-patam starts at 25m (82ft) after you have dropped down a beautiful slope of white sand covered with small coral heads. The drop-offs continue to 70m (230ft) or more. For the adventurous, this area provides some of the most exciting, and largely unexplored dive sites encountered anywhere.

ABOVE *A tranquil sunset over Scott Reef lagoon.*
OPPOSITE *Divers at 25m (82ft) on Seringapatam Reef.*
TOP (left to right) *A banded sea snake* (Laticauda colubrina) – *sea snakes are a feature at Seringapatam; Mozambique scorpionfish* (Parascorpaena mossambica).
RIGHT *Gorgonian sea fans* (Subergorgia mollis).

Tides and rips are not usually a problem, unless you choose a drift through the channels at the peak time. During the season – from about June to October – the visibility is usually greater than 30m (100ft), and the water temperature around 27°C (80.6°F). There has been some coral bleaching of hard corals at shallower depths.

It is possible to dive from May to November, but the best time to visit is in August and September, for still, balmy days and nights. You can fly from Perth to Broome, and the atolls are around a 12-hour journey by charter boat from Broome. The only accommodation around these reefs is on the live-aboard dive vessel.

ROWLEY SHOALS

Situated around 280km (174 miles) from the mainland (approximately 119°22'E and 117°29'S), the Rowley Shoals are one of the most perfect examples of shelf atolls in Australian waters. They formed more than 10 million years ago when the western continental shelf subsided. As the land submerged, the corals grew upwards to form three oval-shaped atolls, 30 to 40km (18 to 25 miles) apart.

Each atoll consists of a rim of reef surrounding a large lagoon. They rise from approximately 400m (1323ft) of water, and their western sides all drop off extremely steeply. The northernmost atoll, known as Mermaid Reef, is 16km (10 miles) long, 7km (4 miles) wide, and has a small sand cay which appears inside the lagoon at low tide. The rim of the atoll is breached in the northeast corner where a wide channel allows boats access to the sheltered lagoon within.

Clerk Reef, some 30km (18 miles) further south, is similar but has a permanent sand cay. Imperieuse Reef is the most southerly atoll. It also has a permanent sand cay where a weather station has been erected. However, only small boats can traverse its channel.

When the first surveys of marine life were conducted at the Rowley Shoals in 1982 and 1983, the Western Australian Museum added more than 340 new species of fish to Western Australian records. One of the most impressive species of fish at the

Rowleys is the huge potato grouper. These fearless, inquisitive monsters often approach divers and even taste outstretched hands and fins.

They, plus many other large species such as Napoleon wrasse and bumphead parrotfish, could easily have been in jeopardy had it not been for prompt action in declaring the Rowley Shoals a restricted area for fishing and specimen collection.

Marine Park status for most of the Shoals then followed. Luckily, this – combined with their isolation (access is only by boat from Broome), and inclement weather during the summer cyclone season (November to April) – has saved the Rowley Shoals from human exploitation and kept them in near pristine condition.

Huge clams, spider shells, cowries, colourful anemones with their associated anemonefish (clownfish), damsels and striking purple queenfish all crowd among prolific coral growths at depths of less than 5m (16ft) on top of the reef. Shallow coral heads within the lagoons support enough life to entertain a diver for hours, while the outer reef drop-offs are simply breathtaking. Every centimetre of the coral foundation is occupied by living hard corals, soft corals, gorgonians, anemones, ascidians, hydroids and sponges. Reef fish from nearly every family are found here, and large schools of trevally, bream, snapper, tuna, mackerel and bonito are often sighted. Reef sharks and manta rays are also common.

Drift dives through the channels of Mermaid and Clerk Reefs are exhilarating experiences. Water swirls you past large coral heads as schools

---

ABOVE *Reefscape with a vivid gorgonian sea fan.*
BELOW LEFT *A diver admiring pink sea whips through a cloud of small fish at Mermaid Reef.*
BELOW *Teeming reef fish at Mermaid Reef.*

of fish simply hover, motionless in the current. Look out for the unsuspecting turtle or reef shark

---

ABOVE (left to right) *A leaf scorpionfish* (Taenianotus triacanthus); *a brittlestar climbs up a sea fan.*
BELOW *A large potato grouper* (Epinephelus tukula) *fearlessly approaches a diver.*

as you shoot around a corner, and watch out for manta rays skimming the surface above you.

Visibility of more than 40m (130ft) is normal during the winter months and early spring, although the water temperatures may be a little cooler than expected for a tropical reef environment. Underwater temperatures of 29 to 30°C (84 to 86°F) do occur, but 25 to 26°C (77 to 79°F) is not uncommon.

In August and September, when there is little wind and the land temperature is a pleasant 30°C (86°F), there is nothing better than to relax after a full day's diving, sitting in a motionless boat, watching a magnificent sunset reflected in the mirror of Mermaid Lagoon. The Rowley Shoals are still one of the world's relatively untouched diving frontiers.

NINGALOO REEF

The Ningaloo Reef is one of Australia's most important tracts of reef. It extends for approximately 260km (160 miles), from the Northwest Cape at Exmouth to past Amherst Point (south of Coral Bay). The reef ranges from between 7km (4 miles) off the coast to less than 200m (650ft) from the shore. It is the longest fringing reef in the world, and its many beautiful lagoons provide some of Australia's easiest and most delightful snorkelling and shallow diving.

Ningaloo is most renowned for its regular visits by whale sharks. It is here that these magnificent fish can be predictably found and studied. The whale shark is the largest cold-blooded animal in the world, and the largest fish. It grows to over 12m (40ft) long and can have a mouth a metre (3ft) wide. Yet it is a harmless filter feeder.

The sharks come to Ningaloo every March and usually stay until June. This coincides with the annual coral spawn on the reef, which turns the sea into planktonic 'soup'. Despite the plankton, visibility is often 20 to 30m (65 to 100ft). Charter boats employ spotter planes to guide them to the whale sharks, and sometimes seven or eight sharks may be seen in one day.

The area was proclaimed a Marine Park in 1987, which is managed by the Conservation and Land Management Department. No scuba or flash equipment is to be used when swimming with the whale sharks, but neither are necessary since the

sharks cruise close to the surface, and snorkellers can usually keep up easily with a slow-feeding animal. To swim with a whale shark is an awesome experience. The gigantic mouth is held wide open as it feeds and you may see it gulp an enormous quantity of water and plankton. The head is usually surrounded by small pilot fish and juvenile golden trevally, while remora are often stuck to its ventral surface. Other large fish, such as the shark-like cobia, sometimes swim close by.

There is, of course, more to Ningaloo than whale sharks. This reef is home to more than 500 species of fish, 250 species of corals and about 600 species of molluscs. Green, loggerhead and hawksbill turtles are prevalent, and green turtles in particular have extensive nesting sites along this coast. Manta rays are common, and occasionally, large shoals of them can be seen feeding on the plankton.

Whale-watching tours are organized between August and October, when humpback whales migrate down the coast. They give birth to their calves in the tropical waters and meander back close to the coast on their way to the southern regions for summer. Schools of dolphins are often sighted and dugongs feed in the shallow sea grass beds along the coast. The entire length of the outer reef of Ningaloo offers exciting diving with huge schools of cardinalfish and baitfish that blot out the reef behind them. As you swim through these walls of fish, it is always a surprise to find the reef ledges harbouring large black stingrays, nurse sharks, potato groupers and a myriad small reef fish surrounded by colourful invertebrates.

ABOVE *Ningaloo Reef, near the Exmouth Peninsula.*
LEFT *A pair of nudibranchs (Chromodoris magnifica) swim over a well camouflaged stonefish.*

Diving over the reef flats and inner lagoons is also rewarding. You may find yourself completely surrounded by thousands of transparent, pulsating saucer jellyfish, or among a reef of anemones filled with Clark's anemonefish, or the beautiful Australian clownfish.

Turquoise Bay is one of the most attractive and popular beaches for swimming and snorkelling. A gentle current very close to the shore carries the snorkeller over a clear, sandy bottom dotted with hard corals, anemones and sponges. Three-spot dascyllus and other damselfish are regularly seen here, as are eels, octopus and scorpionfish.

It should be said that visibility on Ningaloo Reef is not always better than 20m (65ft). In fact, at times it can be as poor as 2 or 3m (6.5 to 10ft). Water temperatures vary from 22 to 29°C (71 to 84°F). Nevertheless, for exciting diving and for sheer numbers of marine species, Ningaloo Reef is hard to beat.

To enjoy the best conditions, you should visit the reef between April and November. The period from April to June is the best time for diving with whale sharks.

ABOVE *A snorkeller is dwarfed by a majestic whale shark* (Rhincodon typus) *in the Ningaloo Marine Park.*
BELOW *A group of trevally* (Carangoides *sp.*) *attack a school of bait fish.*

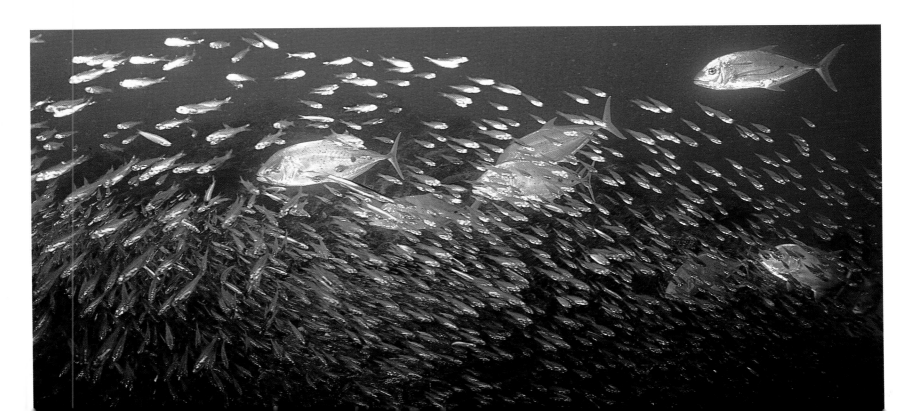

CORAL BAY

Coral Bay lies approximately 160km (100 miles) south of Exmouth on the Northwest Cape of Western Australia. It is part of the Ningaloo Marine Park, which extends for nearly 260km (160 miles) from the tip of the Cape to south of Coral Bay.

The small settlement of Coral Bay comprises a small shopping centre with caravan parks and a hotel. Everything is less than one minute's walk from the safe, calm bay that is filled with branching *Acropora* corals and large *Porites* coral heads. The corals start almost on the shoreline, where children can snorkel near the beach and see a wonderland of small fish darting among the corals.

For the serious macrophotographer, a scuba tank is worthwhile, even in these shallows. Less than 100m (328ft) from the main swimming beach, an enormous mound of *Porites* coral known as 'Ayers Rock' looms from 5m (16ft) to the surface. This may not be deep, but it is a big piece of living coral for such an environment. Fish are sometimes fed in this area, and large schools of sergeant-majors, blue-green chromis, spotted sweetlips, bannerfish, parrotfish, wrasse, and lemon damselfish congregate around Ayers Rock. Wobbegong sharks often hide under the rock, and

the flat coral top is home to dozens of adorable dusky blennies that poke their comical faces out of holes in the coral.

Further out in this huge lagoon, closer to the edge of the outer reef flat, marine life is more prolific. Nudibranchs, cowries, octopuses, crayfish, colourful tubeworms and flatworms, eels, anemonefish and hundreds of other small reef fish are prevalent. Enormous giant groupers (known locally

ABOVE *Sunrise over Coral Bay.*
BELOW *A dugong* (Dugong dugon) *mother and calf.*

as Queensland gropers) inhabit several coral heads near the South Passage – a break in the reef south of the Coral Bay settlement. Large schools of buffalo bream, convict surgeonfish, parrotfish, trevally and even barracuda are often seen swirling at the entrance and exit of this breach in the outer reef, and soft corals and gorgonians line the hard coral walls of the passage.

If you are lucky during your stay at Coral Bay, you may see a dugong. Although there is a population of around 2000 in the region of Ningaloo Reef and in Exmouth Gulf, they are very shy creatures and will usually quickly move away from divers. To see dugong, don snorkelling gear and cruise out in a small boat from Bruboodjoo Point, just north of the Coral Bay settlement. Bruboodjoo Point is a dugong sanctuary where the animals feed on sea grasses in the shallow waters within the lagoon. If you see a dugong from the boat, slowly and quietly slip into the water and snorkel towards it. It will usually be surrounded by a large school of juvenile golden trevallies, which are pretty, small, bright-yellow fish with black bands and dark tail tips – nothing like their grey, adult forms. One or two huge remoras will usually also be stuck to the dugong's ventral surface.

In summer, it can be extremely dry and hot at Coral Bay with temperatures rising to higher than 38°C (100°F). There is very little rainfall in the area, and diving is possible all year round, although the best time to visit is between the months of April and October.

ABOVE *Small fish peer cautiously out from the cover of the reefscape at a depth of 20m (100ft).*
BELOW LEFT *An ingeniously camouflaged tassled wobbegong shark (Eucrossorhinus dasypogon).*
BELOW *Anthias and other tropical fish swim above corals in the shallows of Coral Bay.*

ROTTNEST ISLAND

In 1696 when Dutch navigator Willem De Vlamingh visited a small island 18km (11 miles) off the coast of Fremantle in Western Australia, he wrote in his log: 'Here it seems that nature has spared nothing to render this isle delightful above all other islands I have ever seen'. The Commander named this island 'Rat's Nest' after the small rat-like marsupials that scurried through the scrub. We now call the island Rottnest, and the 'rats' are called quokkas.

Quokkas (*Setonix brachyurus*) are still abundant on Rottnest, and the scenery is as beautiful as De Vlamingh described it three centuries ago. Although it is only 10km (6 miles) long and 4km (2.5 miles) at its widest point, Rottnest is a haven for Australia's flora and fauna. This A-class reserve is also regarded as one of Perth's top tourist venues, as well as being the number-one holiday playground for the city's residents.

The colourful, vibrant marine life inhabits limestone reefs that provide interesting caves, crevices, pinnacles and overhangs to explore. The area is unique in that it supports many tropical species of reef fish and corals that would not normally live so far south. The reason for their presence is a warm band of water, the Leeuwin Current, that circles down from the tropics and moderates the water temperatures offshore. In some of the sheltered bays, hard corals such as *Pocillopora* proliferate, and vivid tropical coralfish and butterflyfish can be found flitting through the kelp.

Temperate-water reef fish are abundant. Western king wrasse, foxfish, leatherjackets, blue devils, scalyfins, breaksea cod, Woodward's pomfrets, banded sweep, magpie and red-lip morwongs, moonlighters, common and rough bullseyes, old wives and eastern talma (or truncate coralfish) are just a sample of the species that you may see on one dive. Large sponges and colourful gorgonians grow on the deeper reefs surrounding the island, while rock lobsters, cuttlefish, octopus and wobbegong sharks are prevalent under ledges and in the caves and crevices of the weathered limestone.

On the underside of the overhangs, thousands of encrusting invertebrates form carpets of colour.

ABOVE *A striking vermilion biscuit star* (Pentagonaster dubeni) *on hard coral.*

BELOW LEFT *King Head and Marjorie Bay on Rottnest Island, near Perth.*

BELOW *Rottnest Island is named after its indigenous quokkas* (Setonix brachyurus), *small marsupials described as rats by Dutch explorer Willem De Vlamingh.*

Map labels: Rottnest Island ○ • PERTH • Fremantle · WESTERN AUSTRALIA · Geographe Bay · • Busselton

These ascidians, sponges, hydroids and bryozoans provide a feast for other carnivorous invertebrates such as nudibranchs, cowries, whelks and many sea stars. Beautiful basket stars are common, and several may be found sitting high up on a rocky outcrop, waiting for night to unravel their feathery tentacles to catch plankton.

Rottnest is also a graveyard for many old ships that struck reefs around the island. An iron steamer, the *Macedon*, and an iron sailing ship, the *Denton Holme*, both struck Kingston Reef in the late 19th century. They lie just offshore from the main settlement. The *Macedon*'s hull is still clearly defined and provides added interest among the caves and colourful ledges of Kingston Reef.

Although many Rottnest wrecks are broken and hard to discern, others are relatively intact, and some are still being discovered. Amazingly, a 50m (164ft) dredge was found – just southeast of Rottnest – in 1997. It rests on a sandy sea bed at 22m (72ft), with its bow rising to within 7m (23ft) of the surface. The marine life living on and around the hull make this one of the most exciting wreck dives in the area.

With wrecks, caves, vibrant marine life and colourful encrusting invertebrates, Rottnest does not need sheer walls and deep diving to be impressive. The terrain is more subtle and the marine life more cryptic. Think small and look closely under the ledges and on the roofs of caves. You will be amazed at the wonderful colours and numbers of creatures that are compacted into every crevice of limestone.

Rottnest Island is a 15-minute flight from Perth, or a half-hour's journey by ferry or charter boat. Most dives around the island are from 10 to 20m (32 to 65ft) in depth, and water temperatures vary from 17 to 24°C (62 to 74°F). The best time to visit is from October to June, although diving can be done all year round. Winter storms and summer sea breezes may lower visibility to a few metres at times, but there is usually somewhere to dive around the island.

RIGHT *A reef scene near Rottnest Island showing an overhang adorned with brightly coloured sponges, ascidians and gorgonians.*

HMAS SWAN

On Friday 13th September, in 1996, the Royal Australian Navy's destroyer escort, HMAS *Swan*, was decommissioned after 26 years of service. It was a sad day for the *Swan* whose possible future as scrap metal hardly seemed to be a fitting end to a proud warship. The Commonwealth Government then announced that the ship would be donated to the State of Western Australia. Endless possibilities arose for its future use: a museum, a floating restaurant, accommodation, and even a church! Finally, the Geographe Bay Artificial Reef Society won the bid to sink the HMAS *Swan* as an artificial reef for divers.

It took hundreds of volunteers, a technical advisory committee comprising conservation and government departments, and a full-time co-ordinator nearly a year to prepare the destroyer for sinking. Every loose piece of metal, every drop of oil and fuel, all plastics, lead ballast and every strand of electrical cabling had to be removed for environmental and diver safety reasons. Access holes were cut into the hull for extra diver safety. These holes also allowed the ship to sink more quickly and to land upright on the sea bed. She now sits in 30m (100ft) of water in beautiful Geographe Bay, 300km (186 miles) south of Perth in Western Australia.

HMAS *Swan* is 113m (370ft) long, 12.5m (40ft) wide and 23m (75ft) high. Most of the ship is accessible, although wreck-diving qualifications are recommended to penetrate the hull. The magazine, the galley, the toilets and the crew's quarters all contribute to the excitement of diving the vessel, but you don't have to enter these areas to enjoy the dive. The radar tower and the crow's nest loom upwards to within 7m (23ft) of the surface, and on a clear day you can see the whole outline of the wreck from your dive boat. The bridge is easily accessible, and is now shared by divers and hundreds of fish that have made the *Swan* their home.

LEFT *A view of the HMAS* Swan *from below, showing a diver ascending past the radar tower and crow's nest, which reach to within 7m (23ft) of the surface. This destroyer escort was sunk in Geographe Bay in 1997, to create an artificial reef.*

underwater, control your breathing for a moment so as to be able to hear their melodious song.

The best place to hear the whales is as you stand on the crow's nest doing a decompression stop. While there, look at the sawn-off ends of the railing. A horned blenny will be peering out at you. Nearly every pipe now has its resident fish. There is no better way to end a dive than by watching these comical, fluffy-tentacled, bug-eyed beauties burping at you with wide, smiling mouths from the highest point of a majestic warship.

Land temperatures vary between 22 and 32°C (71 and 90°F) in summer and 15 to 23°C (59 to 73°F) in winter. The water temperatures vary between 16 and 22°C (60 and 71°F), and the visibility from 5 to 30m (16 to 100ft), depending on weather conditions. The best time to dive the HMAS *Swan* is from February to May, although there are good days throughout the year.

When HMAS *Swan* was scuttled in December 1997, she was devoid of marine life. Within hours, three species of fish were found swimming around her. Within 12 months, more than 60 species were recorded in and around the ship, and many invertebrates including hydroids, anemones and sponges are now growing on her hull. Swimming through this maze, surrounded by bullseyes,

sweep, old wives, eastern talma and morwong, is a wonderful experience. Large schools of samson fish, southern yellowtail scad and dart zoom around the wreck, while an enormous school of globe fish sometimes congregates at the bow.

Humpback whales regularly pass by the *Swan* on their migration to the Antarctic Ocean in spring. You often see them from the surface, or if

TOP LEFT *A diver floats above the crow's nest of the wreck of the HMAS* Swan.

ABOVE *A horseshoe leatherjacket* (Meuschenia hippocrepis), *has distinctive markings and a rough skin.*

BELOW *The HMAS* Swan *has been made safe for divers, with many points of entry or exit, but a wreck-diving qualification is advisable if you wish to enter the wreck.*

NEPTUNE ISLANDS

Just thinking about the great white shark, one of the world's most voracious predators, gets the heart pumping. Imagine what it is like to meet one face to face. White great sharks can be found throughout the temperate seas and many international operators 'do' great white sharks, but because of its clear waters and large animals, one of the most popular great white shark destinations is in South Australia near a sleepy little town called Port Lincoln.

Adjacent to Port Lincoln are several rocky reefs, home to large colonies of New Zealand fur seals and Australian sea lions, both favourite great white shark food. In past years, Dangerous Reef (east of Port Lincoln in the Spencer Gulf) was the destination for great white shark expeditions, but recent regulations protecting sea lions during pupping season forced operators to move to the Neptune Islands southeast of Port Lincoln, just outside the mouth of the Spencer Gulf. Both areas produce good shark sightings.

Boarding a live-aboard vessel in Port Lincoln, it is a quick trip to the Neptunes, and once the anchor is firmly hooked, chumming (known locally as berleying) begins. Those with weak stomachs might believe they would be incapable of sitting on a boat spewing gallons of blood, tuna oil and minced fish into the water, but the whole process is quite sanitized. The magic brew is mixed in a big vat and an electric pump cleanly flushes the chum over the side in a continuous and regulated stream.

When a shark arrives, everyone jumps into cages, which look like huge refrigerators made out of aluminium screen-door material. Floating with the ceiling of the cage on the surface, the

ride can be a rough one, and those prone to seasickness should take tablets.

First-time great white shark divers are always amazed at how peaceful the sharks are. Television documentaries lead viewers to believe that great white sharks are constantly thrashing and ravaging, but this only happens when they are teased with solid bait. Blood and oil attract sharks, but their demeanour is one of curiosity. Having not yet found any solid bait, they simply cruise the area, watching and waiting, occasionally nosing the cages to see if they are the source of the blood.

The whole thing is quite surreal. The cage is bouncing around yet you are loath to grip the mesh of the cage for fear your fingers will be bitten (which is most unlikely). Looking through the windows, you have an uninterrupted view of a monster you have been taught to fear all your life. Every cell in your body tells you to be frightened, yet for some inexplicable reason, you are not. It is quite an adrenaline-rush.

Sometimes the sharks stay for hours, sometimes they stay for only a few minutes, and between dives, there isn't much to do. Dinghies can transfer passengers to the islands, which are worth a visit. They are littered with seals and their pups, offering good photo opportunities.

OPPOSITE TOP *An overview of Port Lincoln in South Australia, a departure point for the Neptune Islands.* OPPOSITE BOTTOM AND BELOW *Divers come to the Neptune Islands to experience close encounters with great white sharks* (Carcharodon carcharias).

Some operators entertain their guests by dropping the cages to the sea bed, allowing divers to watch the fish and large rays that congregate underneath to feed on scraps from the chum. The water is usually clearer on the bottom than on the surface, where all the oil and blood accumulates. Equally exciting is being on the bottom when a great white shark arrives. Seeing these monsters emerging from the distant murk is the stuff nightmares are made of.

Still other operators offer to take divers 'around the corner' for a proper dive, but there are few takers. The idea of diving unprotected anywhere near a chum area, especially in the company of seals, is enough to put most people off.

In the absence of shark action, most people simply sleep, watch videos, tinker with their cameras or read. Strictly for the deadly serious or very rich, great white shark trips are very expensive and there are no guarantees. If you see sharks, then you have had a good trip. If you don't (which is not uncommon), well, there is always next year.

But for those who can afford it, even a single sighting makes it all worthwhile. There is nothing quite like seeing a great white shark up close and toothy from the complete safety of a cage.

The best time to go is during seal pupping season from January through April, middle summer to autumn in the southern hemisphere. The weather is usually fine with only the occasional storm or strong wind. Air temperatures range from 16 to 24°C (60 to 75°F).

Some dive operations offering cage diving with the sharks work from Port Lincoln, some from Adelaide. Adelaide is a large airport by Australian standards and is serviced by standard commercial aircraft. Port Lincoln is a small airport and is serviced by small aircraft, some only holding 15 passengers. Luggage space on the small aircraft from Adelaide to Port Lincoln is limited, and sometimes not all the luggage will fit on one aircraft. If you are travelling with a lot of equipment, consider arriving a day early, thereby allowing time for extra luggage to arrive on subsequent flights.

TEXT CONTRIBUTORS

General Consultant

Jack Jackson is an advanced BS-AC diver who ran a sport diving operation and a diving boat in the Sudanese

Red Sea for 12 years and has been diving around the world ever since. A Fellow of the Royal Photographic Society in Underwater Nature Photography, a Fellow of the Royal Geographical Society and a member of the British Society of Underwater Photographers, as a professional photographer and author Jack writes and photographs regularly for a wide variety of magazines, weekend supplements and book publishers worldwide. An award winner for both his photography and his writing, Jack has written 10 books in his own name including; *The Dive Sites of Malaysia and Singapore*, *The Dive Sites of the Philippines* and *The Dive Sites of Aruba, Bonaire and Curaçao* (all New Holland Publishing), and was consultant and main contributor for *Top Dive Sites of the World* for New Holland Publishing (NHP). *The Dive Sites of the Philippines* won the Kalakbay Award for the top foreign publication of 1996 and *Top Dive Sites of the World* won the Diver Award for the top publication (book, CD-ROM or video) of 1997. Jack Jackson was also the consultant for the NHP title *The Underwater Photography Handbook*.

Marine Biology Consultant

Mike Bruton is the Director of Science and Environment Programmes for MTN South Africa. He is an Honourary

Professor of the University of Cape Town, was until November 1998 the Director of Scientific and Educational Services at the Two Oceans Aquarium, and Director of the Two Oceans Environmental Education Trust, Cape Town. He was Director of the JLB Smith Institute of Ichthyology, and Professor of Ichthyology at Rhodes University, Grahamstown, from 1982–1994. Prof Bruton has conducted research on the ecology, biology and conservation of fish and aquatic invertebrates in South Africa, Namibia, Malawi, Mozambique, Botswana, Kenya, England, France, Belgium, the Middle East, the USA, Canada and Australia. He has more than 100 international scientific publications to his credit, and has presented papers at numerous international conferences. He was the consultant on *The Aquarium Fish Handbook* (NHP).

WESTERN INDIAN OCEAN

PROTEA BANKS, PONTA DO OURO AND THE BAZARUTO ARCHIPELAGO

Stefania Lamberti is a freelance photo-journalist who specializes in underwater and travel. She has written the *Globetrotter Guide to the Maldives* and has contributed to *Top Dive Sites of the World* (both NHP). Stefania and her husband Peter own a company called The Wild Side/Aqua Vision TV Productions, and produce television documentaries. In South Africa, they have a series on M-Net called 'The Getaway Explorer'. Internationally they are currently doing two co-productions – a 13-part half-hour series, 'Blue Reef Adventures', with Discovery Channel; a 13-part half-hour series, 'Dwellers of the African Wilderness', with National Geographic Channel. They have produced one-hour shark specials for Discovery's Shark Week.

ALIWAL SHOAL, SODWANA BAY AND PEMBA ISLAND

Judy Mann-Lang holds a Masters Degree in Ichthyology from Rhodes University and is passionate about the con-

servation of our marine environment. Her interest in fish started at an early age and she began diving in 1989. She is an enthusiastic sport diver and makes use of every opportunity to explore our seas. She is currently the manager of the Sea World Education Centre, where, amongst many other activities, she also runs environmental courses for divers. She has written numerous scientific papers and many popular articles.

BASSAS DA INDIA AND COMOROS ISLANDS

Geoff Spiby is an award-winning photographer who has been diving for eighteen years. His photographs have

been included in numerous magazine articles and books on diving, including the NHP publications *Top Dive Sites of the World*, *The Diver's Handbook* and *The Aquarium Fish Handbook*. He has dived in the Red Sea, Maldives, Comoros, off Pemba Island, Bassas da India and South Africa. Geoff works full-time as a veterinarian in Hout Bay, Cape Town, South Africa, but travels to tropical dive sites whenever he gets the

opportunity. His wife, Lyn, is also a keen diver, and their two children, Kevin and Jacky, are avid snorkellers.

SEYCHELLES

Lawson Wood is an award-winning underwater photographer and author. He is a member of the British Society

of Underwater Photographers and a Fellow of the Royal Photographic Society. He is a also a Fellow of the Royal Geographical Society and a founder of the Marine Conservation Society. He is the author of the recent NHP publication *Top Dive Sites of the Caribbean*, and was a major contributor to *Top Dive Sites of the World*. Lawson Wood has written the following dive titles for NHP: *The Dive Sites of the Cayman Islands*; *The Dive Sites of Cozumel and the Yucatan*; *The Dive Sites of the Bahamas*; *The Dive Sites of the Virgin Islands*; and *The Dive Sites of Malta Gozo & Comino* (with his wife Lesley).

THE RED SEA

Jack Jackson (see above), with the exception of pages 50–53 [but including tinted panels on pp52/53], and 56/57.

Lawson Wood (see above) pp 50–53 [excluding tinted panels], and 56/57 – Râs Muhammad and Sha'b 'Abu Nuhâs.

CENTRAL INDIAN OCEAN

INDIA
LAKSHADWEEP ARCHIPELAGO

Fiona Nichols is a writer, photographer and keen recreational diver. She lived in Southeast Asia for more

than a decade, and her published work includes a guide to Phuket (Thailand), a book on the Taj Mahal, and contributions to several guide books. She was one of two editors of a book on diving in Southeast Asia and one on the marine life of Southeast Asia. Fiona is currently writing guide books to both Mexico and Andalucia for New Holland Publishing.

ANDAMAN ISLANDS

Paul Lees: All his SCUBA diving training, right up to and including PADI Instructor, took place in the UK. During

this time he took time out to dive recreationally around Malta and its immediate environs of Comino and Gozo, the Philippines, Singapore and Japan. His duties as Instructor have been mainly carried out in southern Thailand; namely Koh Samui and Krabi province. His writing and photographic projects allow him to broaden his horizons even further and the list of destinations on his wish list is gradually becoming endless! In Thailand he heads a company called Sun offa Beach which offers a complimentary consultancy and booking service for divers from all over the World. Paul carries an extensive image library for sale and hire.

MALDIVES

Rob Bryning and Sam Harwood established their company, Maldives Scuba Tours, more than ten years ago.

They have extensive experience of the diving in the region having enjoyed thousands of dives both in the Maldives and throughout the world. While they have personal knowledge of almost all the resort islands in the Maldives, it is their time spent on their liveaboards, the MV *Keema* and the MV *Sea Queen*, that has given them access to the more remote dive sites of the archipelago. Rob and Sam are keen underwater photographers and together authored *The Dive Sites of the Maldives* for NHP. They are also regular contributors to diving publications worldwide. They have two young children, Alexander and Ella, who have yet to experience the thrill of their first scuba dive.

CHAGOS ARCHIPELAGO AND SRI LANKA

Dr Charles Anderson is a diver and professional marine biologist who has lived and worked in the Maldives since 1983. He has carried out research on Maldivian reef and oceanic fish, sharks, cetaceans and reef invertebrates. He has written over 100 reports on this research, as well as many popular articles and a series of five guide books to the marine life of the Maldives. In addition, he has dived extensively around Sri Lanka

over many years, and has written a guide book to the island's marine fish. However, some of his favourite diving memories are from the Chagos, which he visited in 1996 as part of a scientific diving expedition.

EASTERN INDIAN OCEAN

MYANMAR AND THAILAND

Paul Lees (See above) wrote *The Dive Sites of Thailand* (NHP), the second edition of which covers the recently opened Mergui Archipelago.

INDONESIA

Michael Aw gave up a successful career in the advertising industry and moved to Sydney, Australia, where

he works as a full-time marine photographer and consultant. His photographs and articles on environmental issues, natural history, travel and technical aspects of SCUBA have been featured in a wide range of publications. These include: *GEO* (Australasia), *Underwater Geographic*, *Nature Focus*, *Action Asia*, *Scuba Diver*, *Sport Diving*, *Divelog*, *Ocean Realm* (USA), *Dive International*, *Aquanaut*, and *Discover Diving* (USA), to name a few. His marine photographs have received awards from several international organizations, including a prestigious Superb Close-Up Award in the 1995 Nikon International Photo Contest. Over 5000 of his images have appeared in various publications and exhibitions worldwide. Since 1989 he has made 39 field trips to Indonesia, diving extensively in Sulawesi, Kailimantan, Banda, Bali, Flores, Alor and Timor. His most recent work, *Dreams from a Rainbow Sea – Maldives*, has been selected as the Gift of State and endorsed by the President of the Republic of Maldives. In collaboration with award-winning film maker Leo Blanco, he has completed his first video documentary based on *Dreams from a Rainbow Sea*.

AUSTRALIA

Ann Storrie (with the exception of pages 158/159). Born in Perth, Western Australia, Ann works as a part-

time animal technologist involved in medical research and as a part-time lecturer in animal care studies at Bentley TAFE, and is also a freelance photojournalist covering underwater subjects. She took up diving and underwater photography

in 1982, mainly to broaden her field of nature photography. Together with her husband Wayne, she became engrossed in all aspects of underwater photography, although nature and marine biology are still her primary interests. In 1984 Ann founded the Western Australian Underwater Photographic Society (WAUPS). Since 1983, she has had numerous articles published in *Scuba Diver* and *Sportdiving in Australia and the South Pacific*, and a few in other magazines including *GEO*. These articles include stories from trips to Indonesia, Malaysia, New Guinea, Thailand and the Philippines as well as the Western Australian coast, plus a few on marine biology. Ann published her first book, on the marine life of Ningaloo Reef and Coral Bay, in 1998.

Rebecca Saunders (pages 158/159 – Neptune Islands) is a freelance photographer and writer specialising in

marine science and ocean-related subjects. Her by-lines include *BBC Wildlife* (UK), *Australian Geographic*, *Australian Natural History*, *Australian GEO*, and a bevy of dive magazines from around the world. She is the author of *Ambon, Marine Wonderland*, and is currently working on a second book, this time about diving in Australia. She is the editor of *Scuba Yearbook/Scuba Adventure*, a diving periodical, and has a column on underwater photography in a New Zealand diving newspaper. Rebecca was the 1996/1997 winner of the Australasian Underwater Photographer of the Year competition, the first woman to win this coveted award.

RELATED DIVE TITLES FROM NHP

The Dive Sites of Indonesia (Guy Buckles)

The Dive Sites of the Red Sea (Guy Buckles)

The Dive Sites of Kenya and Tanzania (Anton Koornhof)

The Dive Sites of South Africa (Anton Koornhof).